ACCLAIM FOI

MW00904870

"For someone who was so close to death, Tara looks at her ....n as simply an inconvenience. She doesn't let it get in the way of her life."
-Dr. Nancy Snyderman, NBC News Chief Medical Editor

"While we all face personal challenges, Tara Fall seems to have gotten more than her fair share. What is most compelling about Tara's story, however, is not the fact that she was able to endure great hardship. Rather, it is how she used it to build a deeper, more meaningful life. Tara's essays are packed with valuable lessons and serve as inspiration to her readers." -David L. Gould, The University of Iowa Obermann Public Scholar

"In a class called Life Design, I listened to Tara Fall's story and was deeply moved and awe inspired. Her humor, strength and resilience in facing her illness is remarkable. My whole class was moved from laughter one minute to tears the next. I have an illness that causes pain and fatigue and was undergoing a multitude of exams and tests when I heard Tara's story. Through her story I saw that you can build a future through any obstacle." -Joylene Beadleston

"Whether you need a shot of inspiration to motivate your day or a fresh perspective on overcoming the obstacles you face, Tara Fall's amazing story and her optimistic approach to life will lift you up and help you on your journey. This collection of her essays is a perfect way to start your day -- a daily reminder to recognize the special things in life that are often overlooked." -Diane Winger, author of *Faces* (suspense novel related to prosopagnosia)

"In Tara Fall's world, everyone is a stranger. Fall's story highlights the resilience of the human spirit."
-John Riehl, Writer, Editor at the University of Iowa Graduate College

"Being the mother of a Type 1 Diabetic child, I sometimes get frustrated with myself. Am I doing a good job? Can I do this? Tara Fall shows me that I can do anything! She is such a pillar of strength and wisdom. No matter what life throws at her, she handles and lives her life to the fullest in a beautiful way. Her displays of such great strength and perseverance are nothing short of amazing."
-Dezharae Robinson, Mommy Blogger, Daringdiabeticsmom.wordpress.com

BrainStorming:
Functional Lessons from a Dysfunctional Brain

COLLECTION OF ESSAYS BY
TARA FALL

NEUROLOGY PATIENT SURVIVING EPILEPSY,
FACE BLINDNESS, AND STROKE

ISBN: 1495326187
ISBN 13: 9781495326189
Library of Congress Control Number: 2014903203
CreateSpace Independent Publishing Platform
North Charleston, South Carolina

For Ana and Kylee, thank you teaching me the most precious lessons in love and life. You both make me so proud.

Acknowledgements

How, in a short acknowledgement, do I include all of the names of people who have helped raise me, researchers whose advancement of knowledge has allowed me to live this full life, and all of my friends who have guided me through this journey? It is too much to say in one page. In order to include everyone, I would need to write another entire book.

There are so many people who have made a positive impact in my life offering me guidance, love, grace, and most importantly, hope. I am so very grateful for all of you. I will never forget that it is your kindness which has guided me to where I am now.

Thank you for helping me discover the strength to stand again.

Lessons regarding...

Introduction

$\mathcal{S}$ome people never forget a face. I will never remember one.

I look into a mirror and see a stranger. My children come to the breakfast table, and I don't recognize them.

I have prosopagnosia, also known as face blindness. I can see a face, the same as anyone else does. But I have no ability to remember it. To me, the world is a sea of unfamiliar faces.

At twenty-seven, I suffered a stroke during surgery to cure my epilepsy. At that point, I lost the ability to recognize people – even those I know best. In addition, I had to relearn how to walk. Fear, uncertainty, sadness, and hope filled me as I took my first steps and faced unimaginable obstacles associated with being a young stroke survivor and being left with face blindness.

Emotions brought on by prosopagnosia are conflicted, but I find humor. During a trip to the mall, I became annoyed with a woman who was walking too close to me. She followed me step for step. She came too close; I moved away. Several feet later, she brushed against my shoulder. When I reached up to push her away, my hand hit a mirror. I realized that the lady walking too close to me was…me. Another time, I was mad at my husband for an entire day when he sent me a photo of him dining with a woman. It was a picture of us.

Of course, there are painful moments. For months, I watched my daughters rehearse for their dance recital. When the big performance day arrived, all the girls had on make-up, tight ponytails, and identical costumes. I could no longer distinguish which girls were mine. After the show they ran to me, eyes sparkling with excitement and pride, wanting to know how they did. How do you tell your daughters you were never able to identify who they were or watch them perform what they practiced so hard to accomplish? How do you tell your children they are beautiful when they understand you do not remember what they look like? You don't have the heart to burden your children with these sad realities, but sometimes you can't help but cry.

I lost the ability to recognize faces, but developed tremendous resilience. My young daughter, just learning to walk, gave me strength as we took our first steps side by side. Her steps were guided by the helping hands of an adult; I was aided by the support of a gait belt. I was once the person leading her, and now I was following her. I did not have time to dwell in bed with self-pity. I was determined to lead her once again.

I had to start anew and for that, I am a more patient parent. I will never forget the challenges that came with learning daily skills I took for granted. Getting dressed, washing my hair, and tying my shoes seemed impossible. Now, I try to never assume simple tasks are so simple for others to learn.

I gained coping techniques that help me overcome countless challenges. I pay more attention to body language. I observe more details of facial expressions. I take comfort in routines. Questions I have learned to ask offer more information than the faces I can see. Prosopagnosia may take away my ability to recognize faces, but it does not take away my ability to find kindness in strangers or develop lasting, true friendships.

I have had a decade to learn and grow with these challenges. I am eager to share my unique story. I now tell my story to audiences around the world. I have written various essays for years and have now shaped them into this book. My hope is that others will find it informative, entertaining, and even inspirational. Through anecdotes, I offer laughter and share tears. Most importantly, I explore the inner strength derived from hope.

This book will appeal in particular to the 2.5 percent of the world's population who suffer from some level of prosopagnosia, because information on coping with a world of strangers is scarce. But the broader message – finding hope in a seemingly hopeless situation – will resonate with anyone who has problems, simple or severe.

STROKE PATIENT

Neither gender nor age will eliminate the chance of having a stroke. A stroke may strike at any time.

Strokes Happen

A stroke - a cerebral vascular accident - can happen to anyone. It can happen anywhere. I was fortunate enough to experience my stroke while in a hospital on an operating room table. The medical staff could immediately notice my slacked face and half-limp body. Regardless of the quick response, when a blood vessel is blocked even for a second, there can be years lost.

Learning to walk again while in your twenties, having a child stand beside you learning to walk that very same week, learning to button your shirt again while finding a new way to get dressed using only one arm – all these can tear a person down. However, it can also reveal an amazing journey. It is not until you have fallen that far that you will be able to truly find the rewarding and amazing view of life from climbing back up the mountain again.

Be aware that a stroke can happen to either gender, at any age, any race, in any person. It is best to know the symptoms of a stroke before it occurs, so you can get help at once. Know the signs: trouble walking, trouble seeing, trouble speaking, and weakness on one side of your body. If you experience any of these, call 911 at once and get to the hospital as quickly as possible to receive the medical attention that you will require. A stroke will create a lot of victims each year and many survivors. Know these signs, so you can get the immediate medical help you need.

My Journey

*L*ate twenties – the years of early adulthood devoted to finding yourself and harnessing the newfound independence you have gained. Late twenties are a time in life when there remain comforts from the past but also a dizzying array of changes for the yet-to-be, fully-discovered future. Shortly before we had our second child, my husband and I, along with our first daughter, made a journey half-way across the country returning home once again. We were welcoming the opportunity to reconnect with family that had been absent from our lives due to distance but never far from our hearts. During this time, my seizures were growing increasingly dangerous. We believed answers would be found soon to help decrease or stop epilepsy's hold on my brain. We held onto this hope until the day I awoke to darkness.

I learned in an instant what some people spend a lifetime trying to understand. The life lessons taught to me at age twenty-seven were amazing, hopeful, and profound. When you fall down, you can lay there in self-pity or work hard to stand again. When you laugh, you can find the voice you never knew you had. When you lose your sight, it is then you can find a vision. When your body fails you, it is at that time you will find the passion in your heart and acquire an inner strength never before known. You will realize those nearest you can save you. And most importantly, when you hurt not only physically but mentally, there is hope that can be found. In the bottom of an empty cup, there are secrets that can be offered: motivation, love, and laughter. And yes, once again, hope.

Lucky is the individual who lives a life with a clear understanding it can end at any time. That soul will live fully and never let go of their passion for life. Lucky is the individual who wakes in the morning and looks around in awe, understanding that this day has brought yet another miracle, the miracle to live yet one extra day and have the opportunity to make a difference for those around them. I had the privilege to take a journey into a world of loss. In the acknowledgment of having lost, a new, rediscovered, stronger life can be found. I remembered hope.

In losing our sight, we can gain a clear vision. In having our physical strength fail us, we can conquer inner strength we never knew existed. In laughter, we can find freedom. In hope, we can find that dreams really do come true. During my late twenties, I learned these life lessons. Usually the quietness in finding peace comes through years of learning and the hard knocks life will hand you. I was fortunate to learn them so young.

I had experiences very early on that can age the body, mind, and soul. I learned to laugh when it would have been easier to cry. I learned to find hope within hopeless situations. With life's gifts, I discovered the wisdom only experience can provide. I was able to find answers I never knew I was seeking. I learned to find tranquility in the personal battles my body could fight. Most helpful though, I learned that in finding yourself, you can find strength that will give you power to stand again. No matter how difficult, each time life attempts to knock you down, you get back up.

I have learned that seizures can not only take moments of time, but complete nights, and sometimes years of memories. I learned that though the brain itself does not feel pain, it can still feel the pressure as a surgeon's gentle hands push a retractor against it. I understand that even when your body is strong a sudden stroke - a cerebral vascular accident - can take away half a body's strength and also the ability for movement, leaving behind paralysis. When you least expect it, life can turn on you, taking away so much of what you thought you knew. I discovered what an exciting journey it is to live not as a victim, but gaining the joys of a survivor. I rediscovered my true power and abilities to find the strength to stand again.

The Day the Wind Caught Fire

I looked at the side of my wrist this morning. A glimpse of red caught my eye. I looked again and realized there was brown surrounding the base of the red line. I looked closer yet, and realized the brown was a long blister at the base of my thumb. It was only then I realized I had burnt myself. I attempted to think of when I was near something that was really hot – or really cold in my perception.

Before I had a stroke, I thought a stroke was an ailment, or medical condition, that affects an older population like grandparents and their friends. The stroke would leave their faces drooping on one side and cause slurred speech or cause their foot to drag as they walked. Obviously, I had a complete misconception. This is one reason I started my blog *Finding Strength To Stand Again.* I want people to know that strokes can happen at any age. Strokes occur due to a variety of reasons and there is no textbook prediction of the lasting effects a stroke will have on one's body.

One lingering result of my stroke is the lack of ability to feel correct temperature sensations on the left half of my body. This problem has lessened slightly with the passing of time. When I was first recovering, I remember walking outside as tiny drops of rain began to fall from the sky. I cannot describe to you the pain I felt! It was as if needles were being pushed through my bones. With each sprinkle, with each touch of rain, the needles deeply pierced my skin. I learned quickly to prevent precipitation from touching me. On another day I went outside and there was a slight breeze. The wind was fire. This is odd because fire only touched the left half of my body. My right arm could perceive the wind as normal. With each gust, the raging inferno would rush through my exposed skin on my left side. I learned quickly, regardless of the weather, to wear a sweater or coat draped over my left arm. If my skin was covered, I would not feel the pain.

My children running up to me with chilly hands to grab my arm still causes me to wince in pain. The rain no longer feels like needles, but it also does not create the pleasant sensation I used to enjoy. I still get confused by cold or extreme heat. One area the stroke affected is where my brain detects temperature sensations. This is no longer an automatic sensation I can be aware of. Our counter tops are granite. I have been known to think my hand brushed against the counter – the frigid sensation registering as boiling pain – only to look and realize the skin is really feeling boiling pain because it is touching the side of a hot pan. I do pay attention visually when I am in the kitchen, but I am only human and cannot notice everything. Maybe yesterday I was too close when I leaned over and blew out the candle. Maybe I was too close to the hot coils when I was lifting the lid out of our dishwasher. I am not sure what caused this blister. It is over now. I just need to always be careful.

I decided to write this essay to show yet another way a stroke can alter someone's lifestyle. I used to have fun splashing in puddles. I used to have all of my eyesight. I used to have more "normal" abilities than I have now. Yet, I am amazed at things the stroke has taught me. Please, remember a stroke is not an ailment that affects only our grandparents and their friends. It is not a medical emergency that hits older people exclusively. The handbooks and guides given out to predict a stroke survivor's outcome should not be one size fits all. Set your sights above those predictions, and remember everyone will progress differently. Each stroke affects a different area of the brain in different ways. Have patience and take time to understand how your definition of normal will evolve. After all, prior to my experiences, I never would have believed that a simple blood clot could change me in so many ways, and I never would have understood that a stroke could make the wind catch fire.

Playing Piano In My Mind – Part 1

After my stroke, I cried two times about the events that had unfolded. Both times I sobbed alone in my hospital room. I needed that time by myself to quietly grieve what had been lost. Once those two episodes passed, I was free to move on and accept my future with great hope. I am still glad I took that time for myself. I am glad I finished the phase of shock and fear. Utter fear. With that released, I was able to pick myself up and focus on all the positive possibilities my future held.

The first time I cried was the night of my ten-year high school class reunion. Rather than spending the night comparing stories with my peers of years gone by, I spent that night alone crying in a hospital bed. That was the first time I allowed tears after my surgery and stroke. That was the first time I allowed self-pity.

There I was, all of twenty-seven years old. Rather than having my hair done up for the event, my bald head was wrapped in a scarf to hide the incision. Rather than partying and dancing, I was wondering if my fingers would ever again move by my own free will. I cried selfish tears. Tears fell for memories of how far I had come and how far I had recently fallen. In the yearbook's question of "where do you expect yourself to be in ten years," I never thought to answer "bald, in a bed, with a paralyzed body and a missing piece of my brain."

Please, do not cry for me. I did not shed tears for long. Actually, my tears quickly turned to a deep chuckle that brought laughter up through my soul. I did not have much. I was no longer able to drive a car. Yet, I figured after a late-night party, my classmates really should not be driving a car either. At that time, I knew I couldn't walk without someone's arms around my waist to help hold me up. A chuckle arose again as I wondered which of my classmates would need an arm around them as they stumbled home for the night. And in the morning, I would not hurt. My world would not be consumed by a pounding headache. I would wake refreshed and ready to meet with my physical and occupational therapists. Yes, I had fallen a long, long way. Yet, I was at an advantage over many twenty-seven-year-olds that night. I had the chance to learn the basics of life all over again and be aware this time that I must try my hardest to never leave a stone of life unturned. Every time I touched a piece of the world, I now would understand the true value of leaving it a little better in case I never had a chance to walk the same path again. In those previous weeks, I gained wisdom I never searched for but would never dream of allowing myself to forget.

Playing Piano In My Mind – Part 2

I started playing the piano when I was so young my feet could not touch the floor. I remember my teacher often telling me to stop swinging my legs and start focusing on my fingers. Following my stroke at age twenty-seven, I was unable to move my left hand fingers at all. Occupational therapists suggested I visualize something I had done frequently with my hands or arms. Sometimes when a patient uses this visualization technique they regain use of the affected limbs faster. Until my stroke, I had still played piano regularly.

At night, when the only sounds were nurses shuffling their feet or the beeping of IV machines, I would visualize that I was playing my heart out. I could hear the notes in my mind as I imagined my fingers easily pressing the keys. I could instruct my fingers on how far to be spaced, the beat at which they should move, and the correct motion of the lifting wrists. I played and played and played. It was the oddest sensation. Sometimes I would feel my paralyzed fingers move. I was thrilled this visualization technique was really working! With excitement, I anticipated feeling those left fingers lifting and monitored how far they were progressing. In my mind, I could feel them lift with every beat. I wanted to tell my doctors first thing in the morning. I wanted to call the nurses and have them come and look. Yet, each time I was disappointed and confused when I came to the realization that the finger movement and all the sensation it drew down my arm was only in my mind. Night after night my fingers remained powerless and still.

As disappointed as I was, I knew to never give up. If only I tried hard enough, if only I played long enough within my mind, my fingers would surely play again. I came to the belief that the only reason it was not working was because my imagination was not powerful enough. If I was able to get in front of the piano, I would have the power and strength to let my fingers fly. I got my wish late one afternoon. A nurse wheeled me down to the rec room. Upon my request, she left me alone. As I pushed my wheelchair to the piano, Scott Joplin's "The Entertainer" was racing through my mind. I knew I could play this song; I had played it for years. It was a positive, fun melody. My right hand took off. My heart was racing. My eyes were shining bright. This was it. Years of practicing were going to give me back my left hand movement. I assisted in lifting my left hand up to the keyboard. Here it was…and then there was nothing. I offered no music. My fingers provided no movement. My mind and body failed me, giving no response. How could that be?

I sat there. I started the song again and again flawlessly with my right hand. I tried. I silently yelled at my arm. I cursed my lifeless fingers. I ached at the reality that was playing out. My eyes filled with tears. I felt gratitude toward the nurse as she leaned her head into the room and silently backed away to leave me alone. I cried for the final time that night. I cried for the dreams that now seemed unattainable. I cried for understanding I could only move my right side – no longer the left. I cried that second time because the only music being played was from the fingers playing the piano in my mind.

I allowed grief, and then I was wheeled back to my room. Stroke recovery did not come quickly. It was not a simple process. I worked hard for it. It took a lot of effort. I still work to maintain progress I have made. Eventually, I was able to make my left hand work. I can no longer play nearly as well as I did before the stroke. However, the music I now play is the most beautiful music I have ever heard!

Homecoming: Welcome Home!

I have been to plenty of homecomings. I have laughed. I have cried happy tears. I have watched daddies see and embrace their new babies for the very first time. Every homecoming I have ever had the privilege of attending has filled me with apprehension, excitement, and eventually peace. The homecomings I have been to have occurred in a variety of settings. Some of these were at airports, some watching Navy ships slide into a pier, and others have been going back to my hometown. Pre-stroke and post-stroke, I have been left with similar emotions each time the big date arrives. The only noticeable situation when these emotions vary since my stroke is when I am heading to my hometown once again.

My hometown has a population of only 3,600. My high school graduating class only had about ninety-five students. We all knew one another. Many of us still keep in touch. After my stroke, I had acquired anterograde prosopagnosia. This meant I remembered everyone's face from before my stroke. Names were easily attached to those faces. For a few years after my stroke, I worked in my hometown and dealt with many of its business owners and friendly citizens I had grown up knowing. I was able to take afternoon walks and say hi and name the people I was passing. That was all a while ago. Since then, many people have changed their appearance. Will I still be able to recognize my high school biology teacher who lives across the street from my parents? Will I still know my children's babysitter when we drive to her house and say hello? My wonderful, previous next door neighbors will surely great me with warm smiles as I stop by to say hi. Yet now I fear I will no longer recognize their faces. Time has passed and age, I am certain, has altered their faces as it has changed my own. I won't recognize these changed faces through normal facial recognition (which I no longer have). Rather, I'll identify them when they meet the expectations I have of finding them in specific places.

I am anticipating a few awkward moments as I pass by these familiar strangers. I will smile. I will readily say hello. Sadly, I will not know them. My daughters will not be able to assist me. They are generally good at this. This past weekend we were visiting a park. An old neighbor and dear friend happened to be there also. As she said hello my oldest whispered, "Mom, there is Miss Rose." But in situations like this with people from my past, I will not be able to rely on my daughters' discreet help. I will recognize the look in the eyes of people passing by anticipating my acknowledgement. My questions will be asked. I will inquire as to how they are and what is happening in their lives. New clues will be gained from old friends. I will listen to replies they share to my probing questions. I will laugh, smile, and pretend I know them. "Fake it until you make it" is a phrase I have adapted well into my life. This homecoming will not be on a pier. This homecoming will not be based on crying family members releasing tears of relief. Rather, this homecoming will be a returning citizen seeking old friends. This homecoming will be relief finding familiar patterns, seeking answers through questions I am ready to ask, and, of course, some extra special time reuniting with my wonderful mother, father, sister, brother-in-law, nieces and nephews and so many others I have never said goodbye to but "see you later" instead.

This is a homecoming filled with apprehension and the usual excitement. Once I work my way back into the community I grew up in, I will surely find the peace and happiness that will leave me content.

Telling My Story

*L*ast week I had the great honor of welcoming some terrific news crews into my home. Both newspaper and television media have visited. I am always awed and amazed when I hear requests for interviews with me regarding the struggles and compensation techniques that I utilize to overcome my challenges.

I never know what to expect when they arrive. I have had struggles in my past but nothing that ranks as newsworthy in my eyes. They come though, and we talk about many subjects. We touch on having seizures in junior high school. We speak of me being twenty-seven and having part of my brain removed only to wake and discover I experienced a stroke. We discuss what it is like to wake up with missing eyesight and the complications that linger when some of the sight never returns. I answer questions about prosopagnosia causing heartache when I cannot recognize my family and the fear that comes when I do not know my peers upon sight. All of these questions are asked with tender care; the answers absorbed with respectful responses.

Upon replaying interviews in my mind, I would have expanded some of my answers. One question was, "With everything you have gone through, how do you find the strength within yourself to keep going?"

Here would be my answer: "I make sure I do not maintain sadness or grieve for all I have lost and have been forced to leave behind. I know I will never again run alongside my children, yet I celebrate that I can walk with them every day and help guide their path as we go toward the future. I may have significant sight loss and no longer be able to maintain any visual image in my mind; however, I am able to enjoy what I am currently seeing. The snow-capped mountains, the beautiful sunsets, and amazing smiles my daughters offer are mine to hold on to even if just for the moment. I have a firm understanding that sight loss does not define the vision you are left to create. I have lost some of my ability to hold basic skills we know from early in life, maybe even a lot of those skills, yet I have gained more knowledge than I could have ever expected. The key for me is not to mourn the past but to absorb the joys of the present and recognize great things are waiting for me in the future. I wake up every morning, work hard for the day, and remember to never take treasures like walking, seeing, and being alive for granted. I have the strength within me because I never forget what I had in the past. I hold no resentment for what I lost. I rejoice in what I now have. I am grateful for every exciting thing I know is yet to come."

Happy Anniversary or Should I Say Happy Birthday?

Ten years ago I found myself facing challenges I never could have imagined. Ten years ago this week, I woke from brain surgery learning I had a stroke during the operation. I was twenty-seven. What was it that allowed me to embrace the challenges faced while recovering from this event? Where does that inner strength and determination come from? I really can't answer these questions. Whatever it was, wherever it came from, is unknown, yet I am fiercely grateful for this drive. I can walk independently now. I can speak clearly without slurring my words. I celebrate doing simple things in life most people take for granted. I do all these things which, not so long ago, would have been unthinkable accomplishments if I had allowed myself to accept the dismal outcomes predicted.

Each year I ask myself if the twenty-fifth of June should be celebrated as an anniversary or as a birthday. Anniversaries are happy days set up to celebrate the joining of two lives. Some might not understand why the date of my stroke would be considered a happy day. It is, though. I have always believed it is only when life knocks you down beyond where you could have imagined that you really learn to appreciate all the beauty life delivers. When you climb the mountain of challenges placed in front of you, this is really when you appreciate the beautiful gifts of life. My life before was happy. And, though it is different in so many ways, the life I live now is also joyfully celebrated. So, rightfully, happy anniversary to me for the day which taught me the true potential to change, grow, and appreciate the gift of living. Each year is a happy celebration of joining my life as it is today and the years that helped mold the strength which allowed me to overcome challenges.

Or, should I say Happy Birthday to me? No, it is not my true birthday in the traditional sense of the word. However, the stroke changed who I am. I know I am not the same person I was before my stroke. I accept that. I recognize and rejoice how I am a different person in some ways. I am stronger. I have more empathy for the difficulties people face. I am more attentive to the gifts life offers. I am more grateful for each and every day I have. Life now is never taken for granted. Similar to an infant in many ways, the stroke forced me to learn developmental tasks once again. I learned how to walk and tie my shoes. I learned how to catch a ball, hold a pencil, and hold my beautiful babies in my arms. I learned these early lessons again with the coordination of an inexperienced toddler yet having the eyes of an experienced adult. Using this perspective, happy birthday to me.

June 25, 2013, the night of my ten year anniversary/birthday, ended with my youngest, an eleven-year-old, making a tent and sleeping in my room. She was sleeping near my bed, and I reached out my arm to rub her back. She turned over and grabbed my hand. She was rubbing my arm up and down, up and down. Constant repetitive touches on my left arm and leg have been painful since I had my stroke. I asked her to stop and reminded her rubbing me like that hurts. She said, "Give me your other hand then." I gave her my right hand. She didn't question it. This is her norm. This is just how her mom is. On this night, we fell asleep with her holding my right hand. I can only hope in the next ten years of our lives we can continue to grow and create as many happy memories of success stories as we've discovered this past decade.

Evolution of Goals: Six Miles and Counting

I have often thought about how our definition of normal always evolves. This past week I was thinking about other ever-changing areas of my life. For example, people's goals are always changing, growing, and hopefully getting grander. My physical goals do just this.

The day after I had my stroke I was told I might never walk again without the aid of assistive devices. From that point on, it was explained, I might be required to depend on an AFO brace, a crutch cane, or a walker to be mobile. In my mind, at twenty-seven I was too young to accept this news. I had too much to do in life to never walk independently again. I set a goal of walking alone. I was determined to achieve and exceed this initial goal. I worked hard. I worked very hard. I was determined to continue with expanding my milestones. I listened to doctors and pushed myself beyond what even I thought I was capable of. This determined attitude and hope that I harbored allowed me to complete a four mile walk four years later beside my two young daughters. The only assistive devices I held that day were the hands of my children. Together we accomplished the Coronado Bay Bridge Walk.

My goals continued to grow. This past weekend I "ran" five miles and "biked" six miles. Now I did not actually run those miles, nor did I go out and ride a bike. Some goals are still out of reach. I used an elliptical because I still do not have use of some required muscles that would allow me to run. I rode my miles on a stationary bike. I do not have the balance to keep a bike upright. I hope to run outside again. I would like to take my kids out on a bike ride without needing training wheels or a third wheel. Today, though, these goals are still beyond my reach. For now, I will stay inside on fitness equipment. I make believe the wind blows through my hair. I hear the sounds of a nearby road and feel the sun beaming through the window warming my face as if I were outside without restrictions. My body may not offer me the ability to reach my pre-stroke goals. I do, however, have the ability to make sure my goals are always evolving. I fail occasionally; sometimes I have to lower my expectations. I may not have the ability to take back all of what seizures, surgery, and the stroke have taken. I will always continue to hope, though, and always take hold of the next opportunity life will place within my reach.

I may never run a half marathon, but at least I can keep up with my children on a beautiful afternoon walk. I may never know a life completely free of seizures, yet my inner strength will not allow medical difficulties to stop me from living a full life. I won't remember your face, but I will remember the kindness you offer me through your support, words, and actions. I dare myself to dream, to evolve my goals higher every time I reach a plateau. I trust myself to not just live an ordinary life but work to leave an extraordinary legacy providing optimism and hope to every life I touch.

Stripes = Success

I think of all of the ways I have defined "success" throughout my life. It's a word which, like so many others, has a definition that evolves with where we are in that moment of our lives.

Success is defined as accomplishing created goals or a set purpose. Once, when I was very young, success was being able to ride a bicycle with no training wheels. I wanted to be on my own, supported by nothing except sheer will. This independence to ride alone on the sidewalk was what I then labeled as my greatest success.

Over the years, my goals changed. At twenty-seven, these goals became simpler but the chance to succeed was seemingly even more difficult. I only wanted to do everyday tasks known to the rehabilitation world as "activities of daily living" or ADLs. I wanted to walk from one doorway to another. I wanted to get dressed all by myself. I wanted, believe it or not, to be able to change my daughters' diapers.

Recently, I heard from a twenty-four-year-old female. Her unexpected, unbelievable success came not long ago when she took a shower all by herself. She was even able to reach up and run a wash cloth through her hair! She, too, had a stroke at a young age. Labels of success depend on where you are in your life.

My most recent success was painting stripes on my daughter's bedroom wall. I measured for the stripe's length and width. Okay, it took several times measuring and removing painter's tape, holding up the leveler again and again and again before pressing down the tape one last time. I found success in all things I did during this project. I had enough eyesight necessary to judge the evenness of the lines where they met on opposite sides of the window. I had the ability to dip a brush into the paint and the strength and stability to hold onto the brush and color the walls. I had the balance to climb a few steps up a ladder. I made my daughter smile as we worked together to reach her goals.

Success should not be defined by others peering into your life. It is not a word which can be fully defined in a dictionary. Success is found in your own head and within your own heart. Believe in yourself. Reach for your goals. Define your own success today.

HOPE

When all else is felt to be lost, we can still have everything as long as we still have hope.

Through Humor and Hope We Shall Heal

I cannot remember the exact date I took my first steps. I can, however, remember the physical therapist's exact words. She instructed me on how to use the crutch canes. She gave me assurance that she would keep me up and protect me from falling. She gave me strict, detailed instructions on how to encourage my uncooperative body to cooperate. She then told me, "If anyone walks by with a white lab coat, stick out your cane quickly and try to trip them. When we are on staff, we cannot trip the doctors but our patients can! Help us out!"

You see, I had lost a lot of my sight then. I could barely distinguish a white coat from a tan wall. She knew that. I could not react quickly because my reaction speed had drastically slowed. She understood this. If I stuck out a cane, she was aware I would have fallen over to that side. She had an understanding of all of this. Yet, at the same time, she also held onto the wisdom that I could still laugh. The numbness created by a stroke may cause our bodies to no longer feel physical pain. Our minds might be lethargically slow as the recovery process begins. For a moment, she took away the fact that I was no longer an independent and strong mom/wife/daughter. As a replacement, she gave me an amazing, unexpected gift. At that moment, in that one instant, she created joyful laughter. I treasured that distraction.

I gained invaluable knowledge in that moment. Even when it feels like all has been lost, when we feel like we have nothing left within ourselves, we can still create a smile which may give way to a laugh. Once the genuine laugh has escaped our unsuspecting lips, we cannot help but feel better. No, humor will not provide us with the sudden ability to produce an amazing burst of recovery; however, it does provide miraculous groundwork from which healing can begin. Find humor, find smiles, and you will find your soul lifting up once again.

The other thing I grasped on to was hope. My youngest child was learning to walk the very same week I was taking my first steps. They picked her up by holding under her arms. Me – I was held up by a gait belt. I held on to hope that I would learn to walk as strongly and gracefully as she would soon carry herself. My oldest daughter was two and a half years old. She could not see over the wheelchair as she tried her hardest to guide the wheels in a straight line. I held strong onto hope that I would soon be the one guiding her and providing direction rather than this tiny girl trying to steer me on the correct path.

Humor and hope can get lost. They can get knocked out of you when life knocks you down so far. It is not always easy to grasp these gifts and rework them back into your spirit. I promise, though, whatever the physical or mental ailment that you may be recovering from, hope and humor can be unimaginably powerful tools to help your body learn to heal again. Using a mix of a generous amount of both of these may create a contagious substance that will feed your soul and help refuel your body. Through humor and hope, we shall all, once again, heal.

From Rags to Riches

Rags to riches can be defined as when someone alters their life to rise from poverty into wealth or from obscurity into fame. However, I believe we can make a much simpler jump. Anyone can find their way from rags to riches. It does not need to be such a drastic jump. It can be a simpler leap from a bad situation into a life of hope and renewed promise. Using that definition, I have certainly found my way from rags to riches time and time again.

Yes, I readily admit I am "that person." I am the overly-optimistic individual who can drive you crazy and leave you shaking your head wondering why and how someone can remain so hopeful and happy. I cannot give you the answer to either how or why. I can only tell you that my optimistic thoughts and goals are completely sincere. They have been my lifeline to help carry me through life's challenges with a feeling of hope and peace. I can overcome my obstacles with optimism. It is this optimistic drive that raises me from the rags life delivers and provides my path to abundant riches.

Life has thrown me many challenges. I have experienced an array of stressors. Due to our military life, we move a lot and often have had to start over again. With each move, I am able to find great, new friends and explore amazing new cities. I have gone into *status epilepticus* causing my memories to be wiped away. Due to my encounter with amnesia, I have realized the importance of recording memories to never allow them to disappear again. I had a stroke while in my twenties and temporarily lost my ability to walk. I recall the challenges my toddlers faced learning this skill, and I had an increased patience and truly understood how to help them grow. I lost some of my eyesight resulting in *homonymous hemianopia*. From this grew a new passion to help kids use their eyesight to read and experience adventures – adventures formed by what written words can deliver. From that passion, I was able to not only reopen a school library but also win a long overdue library makeover. My seizures have now returned. I will not mourn the uninvited, unexpected chaos in my brain. I remain thankful for eight amazing years of being seizure free. I kept my memories and will someday discover the purpose of this trial. Until then, I will hold tight to my family. I thank my amazing neighbors for helping me when I needed it, getting me not only the medical attention I desperately needed, but also taking in my children until my husband could return to our home. The support, the love, and the encouragement I received once again made me understand how rich I truly am.

No, you will not see me on the next list of Forbes billionaires. You will not find an enormous bank account with my name as the owner. However, I have no doubt you will be intrigued by the riches I have found within the difficulties – or challenges – life has handed me. I do not want to continue to suffer physically or mentally; however, if that is what life hands me, I am prepared for it. I will face my obstacles with unending optimism, and I will say thank you for the chance to make something more special out of the inconveniences life has delivered. I have the opportunity to grow from rags to riches!

Discovered Number Quickly Offers Success

Have you ever set a goal and felt frustrated or angry when reaching this goal seemed too elusive? Have you ever hoped to accomplish something either small or grand and felt sad, let-down when you never obtained what you were hoping for? How hard did you really work for this desired dream to come true?

For dreams to become a reality, we must do more than just hope. For a goal to be accomplished, we must do more than write them on a piece of paper. No one who is sedentary will lose six pounds in two months by looking into a mirror with a frustrated heart. No one will graduate top of their class by sitting in study hall and skimming through a textbook while making plans for upcoming weekends. Dreams can only be accomplished through an abundant amount of work and determination. There is no other person or program that will offer you a fast path to success. What is the discovered number that will quickly offer success? This number = 1. This number is You. You are the answer for success.

I once hoped, and begged at times, the other thirty people in my challenging statistics class would provide easy tips and give me answers I could rely on to do better. I silently pleaded that physical therapists would be able to teach me to walk again quickly with less work, little sweat, and no pain. I wished the other people interviewing for the job

I was dreaming of would suddenly change their minds and go home. Over time I realized there was only one person who would earn me high marks on tests, offer progress in walking independently again, and execute enough to receive offers for sought-after jobs. I was the only one who had power to accomplish my set of goals.

No other person will walk into your town or onto your campus, seek you out, and provide everything you may be silently wishing. Yet, what if you knew this magical person was actually nearby? Wouldn't you chase them down, smile, beg, bargain, and plead? If the answer to your dreams were that close, wouldn't you do everything in your power and use all of your focus and energy to win their respect? You would never stop chasing them until you accomplished what you set out to achieve. You would do everything you can because it is visible and obtainable.

You, yourself alone, are able to reach these goals. No mystical person is going to appear. You should never doubt your power to answer your own dreams. You can create the check mark next to goals you've written down. Just like chasing someone else who is holding your dreams, you need to place that same level of ambition and excitement into achieving what you want each and every moment. What have you done today to help get closer to what you are working towards? What have you done today that will create answers to your wishes?

No one has nearly the power to help you succeed as you have within yourself. The powerful number opening the door to success is 1. As an individual, you have the power to succeed. You have energy to head to the gym and make healthier food choices. You have the forethought to join or create a study group before you begin to struggle with classes. You have the ability to start thinking about what small steps you can take daily before your feet touch the ground every morning.

I have goals. These are big dreams. I wish they could be accomplished tomorrow, but it will take time and a lot of effort. I know, however, the joy will truly be mine when my own sweat and hard work help me achieve these dreams. These goals are my own. I will never give up. I have enough initiative to not sit and wait hoping for a non-existent person to come and deliver answers to my dreams. Today I will not wait and lose sight of what I want. Today I am using the power of 1 and heading out to make my dreams and goals a reality. I will discover ways to create my own success.

Education Achievements

$\mathcal{S}$hortly after I turned twenty, I graduated with my first college degree, a bachelor's degree in Psychology. Over the next decade, I utilized my degree and found my way in the world applying knowledge I had learned while sitting in the classroom. Nearly thirteen years later, I returned to school and earned my next degree, M.S. Psychology.

I spent the years between my formal education studying life and creating a wonderful family. I had goals that were made, goals that needed to be altered, and ultimately goals I proudly achieved. Over the years, I thought many times of various professors who had touched my life. Some of these professors always had their office door open. Some were always ready for a long phone call to explain the theories I struggled to grasp. I know I was never an easy student. I was that annoying student who participated only by asking too many questions. "Why was it that way? Who said that he had a deeper meaning? How do we really know that is true?" On and on my questions would flow. Sadly, I was also the student that really did not want to sit and wait for the answers. Rather, I just liked asking more and more questions. I succeeded, though, in learning the necessary information. Thankfully, I do not think I caused any of my teachers to retire early due to the stress and annoyance I created. I completed my final degree with a 4.0 grade point average.

Not surprisingly, I believe I gained the most applicable knowledge in the years between my formal studies. I enrolled in Real Life University and spent a considerable amount of time in the School of Hard Knocks. I learned some amazing lessons throughout these years. If I had to write a thesis it would include:

A one-year-old looks cute stumbling when they learn to walk. When you are relearning this assumed talent, it is no longer so cute to watch. The long looks of admiration toddlers receive are replaced with quick glances of pity for adults. DON'T STARE. DON'T BE FRIGHTENED. HOLD MY HAND. WE CAN LEARN A LOT TOGETHER.

Sometimes, while laughing at yourself, the world will not laugh with you. Rather, the world freezes with discomfort and confusion. People render a pause of awkwardness when trying to deal with the space between your distractions of humor and their discomfort. I HAVE A SMILE IN MY EYES AND GRATEFUL JOY IN MY HEART. LAUGH WITH ME. JOIN ME IN MY HAPPY CELEBRATION.

A catheter left in for an extended time can create the need for you to relearn how to void your bladder. This is no longer a spontaneous action that happens with your control. Even the most basic things in life we tend to take for granted; even the most personal things in life may need renewed concentration as you begin to learn seemingly simple tasks once again. NEVER TAKE ANYTHING IN YOUR LIFE FOR GRANTED.

But here is the troubling thing. I can make an impressive resume out of my formal education as I seek future employment. I can wow and awe those hiring with recommendations I had from previous professors. However, the real lessons that made me who I am today would never work on a resume. No employer would respond with an interview call if I wrote of the struggles I have overcome. Too often we, as a society, see the hardships people have experienced and assume they linger in the tragedy they may have faced. I am thankful I am an optimist. I am thankful for the lessons taught both through school and through life. Never focus on my disabilities, but please always remember that I do have some. And for these challenges, I am truly grateful.

It is only through this education which life has provided that I have become the strong person I am today.

Knowing One Land, Living in Another

We have beautiful views in our neighborhood. Go up one block from our house and you will see a bridge with three arches. Below the bridge is a beautiful lake. Look ahead and you will discover the screeches of joy are coming from children playing in the pool next to the palm trees. Continue looking further beyond our community and you may notice the beautiful snow-capped mountains that line the horizon. And here you have it: two completely separate lands to enjoy for many different, unique reasons. I live in the land of the palm trees now, but I spent a childhood growing an appreciation for the beautiful snowy scenes.

This clear understanding of knowing one land while living in another is a reflection of more than just a location my life has me in now. I live in a world where the majority of people do not have disabilities that can hinder their day-to-day activities. In this world, I appear to fit in well. If you ever saw me, you would think I was as able-bodied as the next 5'2", 30-something mom. I can laugh. I can strike up an engaging conversation with nearly any stranger. I do not appear to be held back by any physical limitations.

But that is not the world I have come to know. No longer do I live in a land of "normal" abilities. I sometimes struggle with easy tasks. You will not notice the number of times I have scraped my knees from falling as I practice walking every day. I often feel awkward when getting my kids from school not knowing if the lady looking in my direction is a next-door neighbor or someone who just happened to catch my eye. Prosopagnosia follows me as I go back to my hometown and feel silly when I have to ask my family who someone was that just spent fifteen minutes chatting with me, only to learn it was someone I attended school with for twelve years! But this able world is one I can blend into rather well. I knew it for so long that it comes as second nature. Whether it is a blessing or a curse, I can hide nearly all of my limitations. It is not my land, but it is one I can appear to comfortably walk through.

After leaving the school grounds, I can go and speak with people who are struggling with a battle of neurological conditions. I spoke with a dad and his daughter the other day. The father had fears of his daughter's worsening epilepsy. The daughter was uncomfortable with the side-effects her medication was creating. They were looking for someone to listen to their struggles. I have been there. I am well aware of both of their hesitations and concerns. I used to attend a low-vision support group. I could relate to the stories of frustration and sadness. These were patients having similar experiences to the ones I had recently passed through. I knew this land. The world of having to acknowledge a disability and pain of limitation is one I am well aware of. I live in this land, also.

And so, from a block away I can see two lands. One is the land of perpetual summer where a pool is always open and the palm trees gently sway. I love lounging by the water and later calling my winter-frozen family to complain about the sun being too warm. I keep looking ahead, and I see a land that reminds me of the past where I used to live – similar to the able-bodied world I still walk through. It would be so nice to go up the snowy mountain and be entertained by sleds and skis once again. Yet, I have a comfort in the land where I now reside. There is a peace in looking around and knowing, as the palm trees sway and darkening sky glows with a bright, vivid sunset, that the warm winds will be waiting for me in the morning.

It is a gift to have experienced so many different aspects of life. I have been able to develop the ability to walk between different lands and rarely feel as if I am out of place. I belong in the snowy mountains and in the warm desert sun. I belong in the world where nothing but motivation can hold anyone back and the world where limitations are not only accepted but also acknowledged.

Tara Fall

LAUGH Even When No Joke Is Told

It takes forty-three muscles to frown and only seventeen muscles to smile.

Laughing at what life hands you is a choice. It is a conscious decision each of us can make. At times, it is a rather hard decision, but we are creatures of free will. With this understanding, it might be better to laugh and smile as a painful situation passes. As the saying goes, sometimes we merely need to "fake it until we make it."

Recently, I was honored to attend the departure of a military group. The USS Higgins pulled away from the pier as family members waved goodbye. It would be months and months before these families would be reunited. There were tears. There were a lot of tears. Both from the innocent eyes of young children and the eyes of the seasoned spouses, painful tears fell. I watched with a heavy heart as the ship pulled away carrying nearly three hundred service members. Each of them left behind the role of a husband or wife, a daughter or son, a father or mother, a friend. But in my heart, I had an immense amount of pride for the job these sailors do. I had dry eyes that morning. I turned to one young bride whose shoulders were shaking as she wept, and I offered that we could turn into the crazy stalker wives. I explained if we jumped into our cars quickly, we could race down to the tourist area of Seaport Village. Once we were there, we could watch the ship as it pulled around the bend. We could embarrass our kids and keep yelling out words of love to the passing ship. Then we could again race to the cars and rush through red lights to make it up to Cabrillo National Monument where we could see the ship head out into the open ocean. I laughed and said, "Up there we could again start yelling at the top of our lungs, 'Can you please come back? Hey guys, hurry home!'" She laughed. There were tears left on the pier that morning as many sailors carried away pieces of their loved ones' hearts. But that morning, there was also a little hope and a cautious laughter offered to the world. It is okay to hurt, but it helps to smile.

Life does and will, without question, knock us to our knees on occasion. When this happens, there are different ways we can handle it.
You could look around, shy away, pull your knees to your chest and
cry. There will be an awkward moment as people watch, but eventually
people will be drawn toward you and offer support. Your other option
is to look around and exclaim, "Hey, how did my other foot just trip
me? That wasn't right!" Laugh, get up and brush yourself off. Sure, your
knees may be bruised. Your ego may have even taken a hit. However, the
pain will wear away. Keep walking and keep moving. Your knees will be
stiff for a while. There may be a slight, lingering pain. But the world –
the observers watching – they will comfortably join you. They will come
to your side not in pity, but in joy. In your hope, they can find reason to
celebrate. You found the strength to stand again.

Every day we have a choice to laugh or to cry. Every day we have
the right to feel sorrow or sadness within our souls. Today I will smile.
Today I will laugh. I hope it is contagious. I would love to see your
smile. Soon enough the bruises will fade, the stiff knee will again bend
with ease, and our families will all be together once again.

After The Storm

"Rain, Rain Go Away" is a song most children learn early on. We
sang it just last month. In a desert area where we rarely receive
rain, it rained for nearly two weeks. We are used to warm sunshine
splashing over our faces almost every day of the year. With the rain
falling, my children were lost. They had little connection to a world
where rain kept them from chasing their friends around outside or
taking daily bike rides. With the frustration of being stuck indoors, I
tried to instill in them that sometimes you have to settle with a small
burden so you will truly appreciate the good things you normally have.

When I awoke from my stroke, I heard intimidating comments
from two different physicians. One said, "We don't know if you will
ever walk again." The other plainly stated, "Once you have most of

your strength back, work hard to keep it. It will be easy for you to end up back in a wheelchair. Next time you are in one, you may not be able to get back out." Harsh statements delivered from both of these men. Statements, to this day, I am immensely grateful for hearing. If they had said, "Hang on for a year. Then you will probably be better enough to walk on your own," I would never have worked hard enough to walk as well as I do now. Their intimidating words encouraged and pushed me to work harder than I ever had before. I celebrated four years later by entering a four mile walk. Those doctors pushed me. I chose to stand up and push back. I enjoy walking now more than ever before. Once you have lost this skill, learning it again gives walking an entirely new value.

My husband is a member of the United States Navy. He has spent many months away from our family. Often, he has left for a deployment which is defined as being away for six month or longer on a particular mission. On one such deployment, we received two extensions. Imagine telling your little daughters, "Daddy is not going to be home for another two weeks." "They have to keep Daddy out now for an additional three weeks." On the day I received notice that his ship would be extended to an eight month deployment, two months longer than expected, I went to the store. A lady behind me was talking on her cell phone. She was complaining that her husband was late coming home yesterday and he would be late getting home again. I heard her say that he was supposed to be home at 4:30. Tonight and last night, they kept him at work until 5:00! She was so angry about this and how it disrupted their schedule. I felt pity that a thirty minute delay would cause such stress, but I also felt a twinge of envy. I would have loved a thirty minute delay rather than the two month delay. Ah, if only this lady could have seen my emails explaining how my husband's boss was keeping him "late." I left that store feeling sorrier for her stress than anything else.

A neuro-ophthalmologist informed me I would probably never get back my lost eyesight. Having this knowledge, I truly gained an appreciation for everything I see. Rarely do I take beautiful sights for granted. It is also assumed that I will not get back my ability to recognize familiar faces. Now I stand and soak in what my eyes are able to see. Even if the image will not stay with me, I know that I still have this very moment to enjoy.

Returning to the rain, I am pleased to announce that we made it through the brutal days of rainfall. We persevered and stood watch by the window until the first break of sunlight fell onto our driveway. Many of my neighbors did the exact same thing. Like a synchronized plan, garage doors all around us opened and children rushed out to stomp in the disappearing puddles as the sunlight once again warmed their faces. Hold on to your burdens. Look at them with a patient, hopeful perspective. Someone will always have it worse; someone will always have it better. My hope is, when you find your way out of your current challenge, that something better will be waiting for you as you arrive stronger on the other side. I know that this has been true for my life. It was even true with the recent rainfall. After all, a double rainbow was eager to greet our families as we raced to stand in the waiting sun. I was left with this one thought, "We are lucky to have rain. For only after this inconvenience, will we be blessed enough to be rewarded with a beautiful rainbow waiting just for us, signaling that we have made it through yet another storm back to the sunshine!"

Coming To My Senses

I temporarily lost the ability to see. At one point, after surgery to cure epilepsy, I was nearly blind. I lost most of my eyesight. I was only able to see a picture hanging in my hospital room through the descriptive words of a hospital volunteer. In an effort to help keep the patients comfortable, volunteers would switch pictures around to different rooms for patients staying an extended period of time. I explained to this kind lady I would not get bored because I no longer had the ability to see what was inside the frame. She sat on the edge of my bed and provided me with an extended description of a photo my mind could create. I never grew bored with thinking of that picture. Her kindness filled a void in the darkness.

For a short time, I also lost the desire to hear. Because of the recent memories of a loud retractor snapping within my skull, loud sounds created extreme discomfort. However, I learned that when the loud sounds of the world are shut off, you can hear so much in just paying attention to the way a person shifts or in the hesitation a person's body exhibits as they walk into a room. In losing my desire to hear, I was extremely fortunate in gaining a unique ability to listen. I wish everyone could learn this skill.

I could no longer feel with the left side of my body. In slowly regaining the ability to judge temperatures with my left hand, I burnt myself more than once. When you cannot see the left side of your body and lack the ability to distinguish whether a touch lands on a hot stove or a cold countertop, the kitchen can carry unrecognized dangers. The sense of touch is still slightly decreased on my left side, the side affected by my stroke, yet I try often to rub my fingertips on denim or cotton in an attempt to see if I can again guess correctly. With my right hand, I relish walking through stores and touching fabrics. I feel like a child out on an adventure of a great learning experience. I am half aware of what it is like to feel normal sensations. Through my intact right side, I try to absorb everything the left is lacking.

Every person has lost something important to them at one time or another. Every person falters and feels lost when they recognize this special something is missing. It becomes important then to not dwell on what we lack; rather, realize the strengths that develop. I am glad that I came to my senses. I am glad to realize that even though you may not have sight, it does not mean you cannot have a vision. Even though seizures stole my body at night, I still had the strength of the day. Even though half of my body was weak, paralyzed, I was still able to lead an intense version of the "Hokey Pokey." After all, I excelled with putting the right side out and shaking it all about. Remember we all lose something at times; however, when that sense of loss has cleared away, what is remaining may turn into our newest prized possessions.

BrainStorming

No Resolution – This Year a *Revolution*

*B*efore we know it, a new year will be upon us. Here comes the tradition so many people try to achieve year after year: The New Year's Resolution. Dream big. Hope for large things. Be careful, though, not to set yourself up to be let down within the first month.

I do not remember the last resolution I made in January. Too often, I am fiercely aware of the fact that these goals are not going to last in my mind. I prefer to set smaller goals. I prefer to be able to mark my achievements in smaller steps.

This year though…this year I am thinking of something entirely different. How about I skip over the grand idea of a resolution, and I dream about a revolution? This revolution that I plan: Turn the words that fill my life into everyday terms people can understand. Write about the hardship and hope which come with living with various neurological conditions. While being honest about the pain, sadness, and frustrations I face in everyday life, I am determined to also explain there is always a silver lining to dark clouds. I want to give people the knowledge they need to move beyond scary things they may face. Being a stroke patient and experiencing epilepsy can create havoc on one's life. Having face blindness and not recognizing the wonderful people you see every day can be challenging. Yet, once these struggles have settled, there are blessings you can find which had likely never before been sought.

I want to let people know that it is okay to dream. It is okay to hurt. And it is even good if you occasionally fall down. Once you stand again, you will find the true strength that was hidden deep inside of you.

GRATITUDE

Take time to tell others "thank you." Start a gratitude journal. It will become easier and easier to see everything you have to be thankful for.

The Gift of Giving Thanks

*I*saac Newton developed three laws of motion. The third law states that for every action there is an equal and opposite reaction. I have always believed this theory can be applied beyond physics to the actions we take each and every day. For every interaction we have with other people, there will be an equal or possibly a greater reaction. For example, your simple action of taking time to read this book fills me with gratitude, and your kind comments cause me to smile.

I attempt to express my gratitude each time I discover kindness in those around me. One of the first days I purposely expressed my appreciation for someone I was shocked by their response. It left a long-lasting impression on me. That day I expressed my gratitude while resting in a hospital bed. I made a list of teachers who touched my life over the years. I listed those I remembered as going well above and beyond teaching the lessons of not only the classroom but also those of life. Thanks to the internet, I could search for their phone numbers. I called all of them I could locate. Some did not remember me, the student who sat quietly and passed through the semesters years ago with little notice. Others recalled me as the one who was always eager to question the theories they were teaching. They all sounded touched and grateful for the call. One voice quivered. I wondered if tears were filling her eyes. Her response implied joy was filling her heart. What began as a way to pass a day in my hospital bed turned into an experience I will never forget. Please, do not wait until you are alone in a hospital bed to have this amazingly gratifying experience of simply saying thank you and expressing your gratitude to past supporters. Take the time to say it to people who touched your life in years gone by. Find a simple, unexpected way to show them your gratitude and let them know the candle of kindness and knowledge they shared with you still shines on.

When I shop, I write down the name of sales associates who display exemplary service. Too often managers are contacted with only complaints. Not often enough are managers called to receive praise. Service workers make all of our lives a little simpler and a lot calmer when the service they provide goes above and beyond what we expect. Kind words acknowledging gratitude in a simple call or a note to a supervisor can fill a worker with lingering pride and happiness.

Handwritten notes expressing praise seem to be a thing of the past. I am not referring to an emailed letter that can be sent out in a matter of seconds (though those are better than nothing at all). Recently, a friend was asking me for ideas on what to get someone who helped her. She was thinking in terms of something small yet meaningful. I suggested including a handwritten letter. Complete with a stamp and all…how many times have you had the privilege to smile when a handwritten note shows up in your mail box?

Sir Isaac Newton showed us that every action will cause a reaction. I hope you experience the joy of showing gratitude. When you offer a smile, when you offer a thank you, I hope you become awed at the reaction this sincere thankfulness will cause. Unexpectedly, the warmth may again travel back to you. After all, we are all like a simple candle helping to light and warm the world around us.

Dance in the Rain

I spoke with a gentleman today. He explained that his family had been talking about me this weekend. He went on to say he even told a few friends about my attitude. He wanted to tell me thank you. Nothing can be more of a compliment for me than having stories I share retold and having someone say my life has made a positive impact on theirs.

I first met this man in a community reading room I go to often. Our encounter went like this:

"Good morning. How are you doing?" he asked.

I replied, "I am great. My groceries were a little heavy to carry home, but it was a nice walk on this cloudy day."

He looked up from his paper and asked, "Why didn't you drive? That's a long walk!"

I smiled, prepared for this familiar response. It is three miles round trip. "I don't like to drive. It is a good walk for me. I prefer getting the exercise."

The corners of his mouth slipped down. "Let me give you my number. Wow, I didn't know you walked everywhere. You didn't get caught out in the rain did you?"

"Yes," I said. "Thankfully it was before I had my groceries though. Besides, it was not rain, it was just a heavy mist. I guess that would be considered rain here in California." I laughed at the jab I made regarding this state.

His frown slid further, "Now I feel really bad you walked. Gosh, that is horrible. Too bad the sun just came out now. It would have been nice if you walked in the sun."

I knew he was making the same mistake so many others unknowingly make. I looked him in the eye and explained the reality of my life. "See, you frown because you think I had to walk to the store. I smile because I know I have the ability to walk to the store. You think I was stuck walking in the rain. I think I was lucky to have the opportunity to dance in the rain."

He looked at me with an awkward smile. My display of optimism is not accepted by everyone. My thoughts of hope and the way I embrace the reality of my life is hard for some people to understand. Yet, I want to share this optimism. Not everyone will listen. To those that do, I am grateful for their time. For those that let me know my story is touching them in some way, my gratitude can never be fully expressed.

After our conversation, he went back to his paper, and I opened my computer. When he packed to leave, I told him I hoped if it drizzled again this afternoon he could take the time to go out in the rain and see how good the warm mist felt. I hoped he danced in the rain. I hoped he would have an opportunity to get out and discover all the joys to be found on this beautiful day.

Today I learned these simple words touched his life; this was a successful day. These conversations brought to mind a quote I found last week. This quote was a perfect summary of a long walk to buy groceries and a small chat that helped someone realize the simple gifts life can offer:

"Life isn't about waiting for the storm to pass. It's about learning to dance in the rain!"

RSVP Immediately

I received an invitation to a great, lifelong party. Now, let me explain that this party was not a quaint little gathering of a few friends to sip tea and speak of simple subjects. No, not at all. This was a party that would last throughout the night and well into the next few days or even weeks! I remember clearly this party was set to begin late on a Wednesday afternoon. The unspoken rumor was it may last for a very long time. If I was really into it, I could continue this party for months, even years. This invitation was not delivered with confetti and streamers. I did not receive an invitation delivered with a quaint lace envelope. Rather, I was presented this invitation in a darkened room with a bed pan and a wheel chair. Four hundred sixteen weeks ago no one really expected me to RSVP. My lingering attendance was merely expected by some of the world. It was silently assumed I had the right to join the International Pity Party.

The day I had my stroke I made an instantaneous decision. I did not politely say I would not be attending. I did not use the manners I had been raised with and explain to society I would stop by to acknowledge my place in the Pity Party before I went off to meet other obligations. Rather, I turned my back swiftly, forcefully and never looked back. No, of course, that was not a literal statement. I was still paralyzed. I did, however, turn my mind away from the victim perspective and offered up my mind, body, and soul to bring on the greatest fight of my life. That was the best subconscious choice I have ever made.

The day I made that choice I felt like a boxer in the ring. My supporters did not hold signs for me. Better than any sign they could have made, my supporters held hope. That is a gift that cannot be measured and cannot be forgotten. Like a boxer, I was in for blows. Having a stroke when you are twenty-seven is not something planned for. When you graduate from college, you do not expect less than ten years later you will no longer be studying statistical equations. Instead, you will be studying just how it is your daughter is better at buttoning a shirt and walking than you are. I captured success in immeasurable equations. I learned to scan walls as I walked down the narrow hallways, so I would not bump into anything. I fought my sight loss. Again, I had blows as I learned my brain damage had taken away my ability to recognize faces. Success again tasted sweet as I swallowed my last Keppra (an anti-epileptic drug I had taken for years). It continues to be a great success as I share information of what it is like to survive brain injury and explain my coping mechanism used to assist with prosopagnosia. There are still blows onto my bruised body. In April, I suffered my first major seizure in nearly eight years. Regardless, the Pity Party invitation will still not be accepted.

I have placed the invitation somewhere deep in the back of my mind, somewhere within my closet of memories. I am sure between my head wrap that covered my shaved head, behind the dusty leg brace I refused to keep on my shrunken leg, and maybe below the cane I have covered with my unused arm brace, you will be able to find that invitation. I hope you don't, though. Never come seeking it.

As I draw upon my eight year mark in surviving and thriving, I have a secret to share for my long-lasting, much-celebrated recovery. That secret? My secret is Hope. Hope is something you will not find in a prescription from the doctor. You cannot discover it when crying day after day hiding in a dark room. Rather, you will discover it when you find the love in friends and family. You will overflow with it when you wake up and acknowledge the gifts that remain and you replace bitterness with an attitude of gratitude. Hope is rarely an instantaneous finding. Nonetheless, it is there. It is in all of us. For those of you who have shared hope with me, I am so very thankful you are in my life. For those of you considering the RSVP to your own Pity Party, I hope you choose to decline. Remember: happiness and love will come into the life you have discovered you truly love to live. Celebrate and love this life!

⌐

5 Steps to an Attitude of Gratitude

1. Begin a gratitude journal.

Every night before you lay your head on the pillow or flip on the television to unwind, pick up a pen and paper and write down five things that happened during your day for which you are thankful. Are you running short on gratitude ideas? You woke up. Someone smiled and nodded at you today. The door was held open for you. You had the opportunity to make someone else a little happier. You had clothes to keep you warm. These notes of gratitude do not need to be extensive. At first, it may be hard to see through the struggles of the day. Persevere and soon you will find yourself noticing the good incidents. In turn, you will become less focused on negative actions.

2. **Stop. Enjoy this moment.**

Yesterday is gone. You can prepare for but not predict and control tomorrow. Enjoy today. It is your gift. Focusing on moments of embarrassment or regret from the past will not help you achieve any goals. We learn from our mistakes, but remember it is important to leave those mistakes behind and only take the lessons with us. When we place all of our thoughts and hopes on the goals and dreams of our future, we tend to neglect the beauty contained in today. This day holds so many possibilities for us, we sell ourselves short to only dream of tomorrow. Enjoy today and all that it has to offer.

3. **Slow down. Relax. Breathe.**

We, as a society, rush too much. We are late to this appointment or have to hurry to the next meeting. The weekend is booked solid between all of the activities we have. Find ways to slow down, relax, and breathe. Hang up the phone earlier. Maybe skip your afternoon talk show. Take time for a walk. Feel the sun shine upon your face. Rather than thinking of silence as being unbearable, relish in the opportunity to just be at peace. For a few moments, enjoy not needing anything and not being needed by anyone. Take time to have the center of your attention be the quiet, peaceful moment of being alone. Each day, if only for a short while, take time for just you.

4. **Write one thank you letter each week.**

Have you ever had horrible service, gone home and posted online or written a letter to complain about what you experienced? How many times have you gone on-line, written a note, or made a phone call to praise the service that you received?

Going to your mailbox and finding a pleasant, handwritten letter has the ability to put a smile on anyone's face. Next time you have the opportunity to observe above-average service, take the time to sit down and write a note to the business. Think of the impact that you can have on the worker. In sharing your gratitude, you cannot help but receive an increased level of happiness.

5. **Relish in the simple pleasures.**

As a Navy wife, I always dole out this advice. I tell people not to focus on when their spouse has to go away. Don't stress about the months ahead where you gain, once again, the role of single person/parent. Rather, take these moments to truly focus on the simple treasures life has to offer. Maybe your loved one laughs with uncomfortable confusion when you lie in bed crying over a good book. When you have that time to be alone, pick up that book and cry to your heart's content. Who could refuse such a good book? When the table is set for one less person, who is to request a big meal? Popcorn and apples are winners on our quiet nights! Find what makes you smile inside. Find what can bring you inner happiness and take time to enjoy that simple pleasure. Whether you want to wake up early and get the morning paper all to yourself or you stop from your busy day to join a friend for coffee, enjoy the simple gifts life has to offer. The effort you place in finding your simple pleasure will be returned as you grow in happiness exploring your attitude of gratitude.

In this essay noted for giving thanks, I want to take the time to thank all of my faithful readers. My heart grows with gratitude and my soul expands with hope as my message is shared to more and more people. I am grateful you took the time to read my lessons!

I Am Rich!

I am rich! Oh gracious, I have recently realized how rich I truly am! Now, let me warn you before you strive to find my bank account number, all of this wealth is neither held in the bank nor will you find piles of gold in my home. No. During this past season of giving thanks and recognizing gratitude in everyday joys, I realized the true wealth that surrounds me. Every night, I go to bed under warm covers with a roof over my head. Every day, I awake to my husband and two beautiful daughters. These children will sing with me. They like to dance with me. These children return to me the abundance of love I provide to them. I laugh and cry with great friends who allow me the privilege of sharing my life with them. I still fall down occasionally; however, I have gotten up one more time than I have fallen. I am still on my feet and standing strong.

Too often we measure wealth with our ability to keep up with the possessions of those around us. Maybe, just maybe, in the weeks following the American tradition of Thanksgiving, we can hold onto these thoughts and relive pleasant memories. Hold on tight to the simple things for which we are grateful.

No, my bank balance is not extraordinarily high. Selling all my possessions will not make me gain recognition on the Forbes list of top money makers. Yet, I am fortunate enough to recognize the true value of the wealth that surrounds me. As I prepare to walk to school to pick up my children, I will smile as the warm sun shines upon my face. I will walk home caught in the realization of my great fortune of having my daughters walk beside me. Into my memory, I will record the stories they share on these daily walks. Their stories are worth more than any book I could ever find. And I will, lucky for me, continue to recognize the true wealth that I possess within my heart and my life. Let's not end this season of giving thanks merely because of the date on our calendar. As the Christmas holiday rolls around, make sure to take time to spread extra messages of caring, love, and offering gratitude to those in your life that make you wealthy, too!

LIFE LESSONS

The world is ready to teach you.
Listen to lessons it will share.
Gather all you can be taught.

Children Just Know

How do you tell your kids you forgot how to walk when they were just learning this essential skill? How do you tell your children that your jokes about hollering for them to come here when they are already standing quietly on your left are not to make people laugh, rather to lessen the uncomfortable reality of not being able to see them? How do you tell your kids you cannot "watch this neat new trick" because you get confused when there are too many kids on the playground equipment at a busy park? How do you tell them all of this? You don't need to. They already know.

I fretted at first about how to explain to my children that mommy had some inescapable weaknesses. It wasn't that I did not want to run and play tag with all the kids and fun mommies. It was just that I couldn't. I did not want to confuse or concern my daughters. I did not want anyone, especially them, to have to help me adapt and carry the burden my stroke had left behind. Yet, I wanted them to be aware that I did not stand on the sidelines because I was bored. From there, I could see their eyes shine so brightly as they played, it nearly caused my heart to burst with happiness. It was important they knew I no longer had the physical ability to join in their fast-paced games, but I was still passionate about watching them run and play.

A friend recommended I find the book *One Foot, Now the Other* by Tomie dePaola. It is a book about a grandpa who had a stroke. The young grandchildren help him learn to walk again. I attempted to read it to my daughters. At their ages, they found little interest or parallel to their lives with this story. My children rarely asked questions. I began to understand this "need" to give them an explanation of a mom on the sidelines was *my* need and by no means *theirs*. I backed away from this hunger of trying to inform them about the how and why of my physical limitations.

They understood though. They told others their mom limps because she had a "stoke" (not a typo, just a word they used in the first few years of comprehending my condition). I did not correct them. I answered the few questions they have had in passing conversations. Then there was the memorable moment when I truly comprehended how much more children understand than we give them credit for. I was invited by Nine News Australia to bring my daughters with me for an interview regarding prosopagnosia. Initially, I was very hesitant. Never before had I explained to these beautiful children that I had never, nor would ever, be able to remember what they looked like. I finally decided it was an appropriate time to tell them. This interview was important for my children, for us as a family, and for others with face blindness. It offered us an opportunity to educate many people.

We sat down and had the conversation in their rooms. Separately, I explained that their mommy could not recognize them. "Yeah," they each said with obvious unconcern, "that's how you have always been." You see, this is the mommy they knew. I am flawed. Every person is. No one is perfect, but these two have known no other Mom. They do not know what it is like to have a mom without prosopagnosia who knows their faces. I may not recognize them; nonetheless, I am the mom that loves them deeply and always cares about and for them. It seems natural to them that hemianopia causes me to not see them when they are standing next to me on my left. Most important to me, they really do not care about these flaws.

This is what they care about; this is what they know. I do the best job I can each and every day. This effort and unconditional love is what matters to them. The rest of this stuff, the things I feel a need to explain to them, this is just for the purpose of removing a burden from me. In no way does this aid my children. Besides, they are growing up quickly. I do not need to tell them much any more. These smart little girls are quickly evolving into the stage where they believe they know everything anyway!

New School Year, Same Returning Fear

*M*y children were anxious for their first day of classes. Elementary school has been a wonderful experience in their eyes. They talked fast and walked quickly as we headed for the playground, so they could line up next to their new teachers. They gave me a kiss on the cheek. Both girls told me I did not need to stand in their lines, but asked if I could stay in the school yard. They took off with their shining eyes filled with excitement searching for friends. I stood in the back, lonely and worried. I wished someone were there to hold my hand. The schoolyard and playground are two of the scariest, most intimidating places for me to be standing alone.

I am a very social person by nature. I am excited to talk to you about my weekend. I want to hear the stories you are ready to share. I have met many great parents while waiting for the dismissal bell to ring. I never see them again due to the lack of facial recognition prosopagnosia has caused. I lost friends I never had the chance to get to know. How do I make someone aware I will not recognize them if we meet again at the end of the day, or even if we see each other a few minutes later? If you are standing next to me on my blind side, I may not know you are there. How do I get them to accept this without the long story of epilepsy surgery in which a small piece of my brain was taken out leading to a brain injury developed from a stroke? I talk with parents. I laugh with parents. At the end of the day, I will walk right past these same parents because they changed their clothes.

My kids have been invited to birthday parties. Epilepsy has taken away my privilege to drive. My children point out the birthday child's parents. "Go ask them if I can get a ride," my daughters urge. I would do this. I have done this. Inevitably the conversation evolves to questions of why I cannot drive. I have seizures. My children are happy to add that I can't see well either. Oh, and they further add, you have to say hi to her because she can't recognize anyone. Most parents are kind about this. Then it comes to my daughters inviting these friends to our place. Would you let your kids go to someone's house that has seizures and suffered from brain damage? I hope you would, but I would not fault you for not allowing this. Brain injuries, epilepsy, having no ability to recognize people – all of these are hard enough to comprehend when they are part of your life. I can only imagine the misunderstanding that comes when you have never met a mom with any of these conditions, let alone all of them. Ignorance can lead to fear.

I am that mom standing alone waiting in the schoolyard or sitting off to the side in the playground. I am not antisocial. Actually, I am quite the opposite. I want connections with people I see every day. I want to know the parents of my daughters' friends. I want to know you. I am apprehensive to say hello because I may have just asked how your day is going once or twice already. I don't want you to judge my repeated, well-meant question as odd behavior. I don't want you to focus on my injured brain before you get to know my healthy spirit.

I am that mom standing alone quietly waiting in the schoolyard. I just happen to be waiting not only for my children but also for a new friend to hold my hand and reintroduce me to others. If you see me, or any other frightened mom like me, please walk over and say hello. It is not always the young children that fear the strangers and the newness of school. Sometimes it is us adults, too.

When No Pictures Remain

*O*n June 25, 2003 I woke up having had a stroke. I lost my eyesight. A very kind hospital volunteer sat on my bed early on during my recovery. She described in great detail the picture hanging on the wall. She taught me a life-changing lesson: You do not have to see images to realize the beauty which fills the world around us. She also allowed me to understand there is a large difference between having eyesight and having vision. Images can be discovered in different ways and vision has more to do with the hope for our future rather than what our eyes see in briefly passing moments.

Getting back the eyesight I have now was a long, gradual process. Half my world is still completely black. I have hemianopia and can no longer see anything using my left peripheral sight from both eyes.

Though I did regain fifty percent of what I can see, my visual memory never returned. The stroke permanently destroyed that piece of my brain. When I close my eyes and try to remember what something looks like, I can no longer create pictures within my mind. Whether I am trying to remember what a sunset looks like, trying to picture a glass of water, or trying to imagine what a tree looks like, I cannot create any mental image or color. The visual memory loss took away my ability to "see" anything when I have my eyes closed.

Yet, as I said, I did regain half my eyesight. At first, I could not see anything with my eyes open, and I was unable to see anything when I tried to remember what I had seen previously. For too long, my world was dark. The world seen through my mind was always completely black.

Yet, through this experience, I have been able to learn an important lesson. I hope you can take something away from this, too. What is in front of you right now? Whatever you see when you look out into the world today, treasure it. Don't take that streak of lightning, the smile from a stranger, or images you may see every day for granted. One day this image may be erased from your memory forever. Regardless of how long or how often I am given to experience any sight, I try to treasure it.

I try to notice all the images and colors which fill my world.

I try noticing minute details such as how a ripple of water can dance with the fading light.

These are images I see with my eyes nightly from my backyard. For three years, I have enjoyed watching the beautiful night sky where I live. I realize at times I am fortunate to still have so much eyesight missing. You see, every second of every day I have this reminder to never take for granted the beautiful world in which I live. I always remember that early lesson I was taught – just because I can't see something or memories do not remain does not mean the pictures surrounding me are not filled with beauty. I celebrate and treasure what I see, even if it is only for a fleeting moment.

At the end of the day, I might not be able to remember sights I saw. At the end of the day, I know there are beautiful things I have missed. Yet, if at the end of the day, I go to bed knowing tomorrow I will be given the chance to wake and see this all again, how could I have any regrets in today?

Pictures No Longer Worth 1,000 Words

I have a picture hanging in my house. It is a piece created by the Australian-born artist, Pete Tillack. Please, take time to look up his incredible art work. I think my "Silhouette Bay" is one of the best paintings I have ever seen. How do I know this? How can I define it as "the best"? Because I cannot tell you what it looks like when I am not in front of it. In order to describe anything besides the fact it uses a very nice shade of blue and has a water scene, I need this painting directly in front of me. Otherwise, I do not have the visual memory to tell you anything about the picture. Yet, every time I see it, I am awed by the beauty it captures.

And no, this painting is not new to my home. I was in love with it from the moment I first saw it at an art walk in 2009. After we purchased it, I spent evenings dancing to "Sitting on the Dock of the Bay" with my daughters beneath this picture. When we moved to our new house, I picked the shade of blue paint on my walls just to match this painting and devoted an entire wall to paint a frame especially designed to hold "Silhouette Bay." I spent hours and hours looking at this painting. Yet, when I step away from it, I cannot begin to tell you what is in this picture besides water and calming blue paint.

Still, every time I see it I feel a slight sense of recognition and an amazing awe over its beauty. For me, that explains why I feel it is the most beautiful picture ever created. To see something for the first time every time and still have it strike me as magically beautiful is a true definition of beauty. I no longer have a visual memory. I cannot hold details of images within my mind. Maybe it is linked to the *fusiform gyrus* area of my brain. It is certainly something deep within my brain. Regardless, I am fortunate to have my daughters' beautiful smiles to see each day. I consider myself lucky to continually discover the splendor of the view of the mountains we live near. I am forever grateful for the unexpected sights of beauty that capture my attention on a daily basis.

I see all of these images as if for the first time every time I see them. For this reason, I am blessed to be surrounded by such amazing pictures that no longer can hold 1,000 words for me. Rather, with each time I see this picture, a child's smile, or the snow-capped mountains, I am filled with a thrill that amazing beauty can exist so close to me. No, pictures no longer can tell a story I will later recall, but I am fortunate that each time I see the beautiful things surrounding me, I can observe, with new-found delight, the beauty which they possess.

See With No Pictures & Hear With No Sounds

I was asked a terrific question during a recent classroom visit. I spoke about a volunteer who described a picture which was hanging on my hospital wall during the time when I had no eyesight. I told everyone how beautiful this picture was. This lady taught me we do not need any eyesight to see the beautiful pictures our world offers. Later, after learning I also lost my visual memory which causes me to no longer be able to see images in my mind, a student asked how I was able to "see" in such great detail the picture the volunteer described to me. I answered her question. However, I did not feel my answer was adequate. This is one reason I love being asked questions. It forces me to look deeper into my condition and help everyone – including myself – learn more about how my damaged brain works.

So, how is it the volunteer could create such an amazing image for me when I was blind and unable to conjure up pictures in my mind? My more detailed answer to this question: Have you heard Mozart's 65th symphony in B minor?

Let me describe it to you: First, there is silence. A bassoon begins to make the only sound. This bassoon sounds lonely, almost haunting, as it repeats the same note slowly, holding it longer and longer each time in between lengthy breaths. Finally, when you are certain the player has no air left, the tuba joins in, adding its low call begging to break the painful bassoon beat. The trumpet joins with the tuba. Their sounds come together becoming almost inseparable. Other brass instruments join in beat by beat. The lonely, slow bassoon sound is nearly forgotten as all the brass begins to play together. Suddenly you become lost in the horn sounds. Their beat becomes more frantic. You listen more closely. Children suddenly look around anxiously. You can't pull yourself away from the horns. Drums add sounds like marching feet finding a battle. The noise becomes chaotic. The rhythm is lost. Its raging speed is frantic. Suddenly: CRASH! A cymbal crashes, destroying and stopping all other sounds. The noise ends, leaving complete silence. Silence fills the stage and the room. Nothing is heard as everyone holds their breath. The heart-pounding crescendo you just experienced leaves confusion, having been stopped so abruptly. Then one lonely piccolo gently breaks the silence. A sweet, long pitch fills the fragile air. Three flutes follow. The dark noise which built to silence is now filled with peace. You feel light as the flutes beckon happiness. The clarinets join and you feel swept away. Chaos, anxiousness, is replaced with happiness. Do you feel what the flutes are offering, the peace?

Can you feel the emotional pull we have just danced through? But Mozart never did compose a 65th symphony in B minor. You would have never heard that piece. Unless you have studied music at great length, you cannot identify the sounds and the feelings this combination of instruments could create. Yet, if you were told this story with dramatic voice intonation, your heart could race. You anticipate what would follow the crash of the cymbals.

Just like I no longer have the ability to see pictures in my mind, you did not have the ability to hear the full symphony. In the end, we all have a similar experience. The picture was described for me so my memory could assist my emotions in creating a wonderful image, if not for me to see, at least for me to feel. This is a symphony you will never hear, yet I hope it made your pulse race. It can leave you wondering the rest of the day how words leave you in awe over a beautiful sound you will never be able to hear. The hospital volunteer left me seeing a beautiful picture. I hope I leave you hearing a beautiful symphony. I truly believe it is possible to see without having any pictures and to hear without having any sounds.

I Laugh, I Cry, I Smile

I have been entertaining visitors for the past two weeks. I am fortunate to have such wonderful friends and family come spend time with me. After two weeks of not writing, I was having trouble coming up with a topic until I stumbled on this idea yesterday. I stumbled, literally. It seems at least once every six months I fall down while I am walking. These are not subtle stumbles where I catch myself and get up quickly. No, these are the stumbles where I fall and find myself flat on the ground wondering if something is broken and then limp for the next several days. Yesterday was one of those falls.

I try to walk three miles every day. I like to be out in the fresh air and continuously try to improve the strength I have worked hard to develop since my stroke. Yesterday was a wonderful morning. I was enjoying the crisp air. I was feeling very good until I had cars stop for me and was suddenly surrounded by others out for a morning stroll. You see, my left toe dropped as it sometimes does when I am beginning to tire. I was stepping up but caught the curb with the front of my shoe. I twisted quickly as I fell and landed on my bum and back. People were asking me if I was okay and whether I could stand on my own. One lady opened her car door and asked if she could give me a ride home. I put on a big smile and graciously declined her offer. I thanked the man holding my arm as I stood and insisted I was just fine. I smiled, nodded my head at the people watching, and attempted to assure them I was okay and not hurt as I quickly walked away. I was fast in my departure, being much too bull-headed to admit the pain and embarrassment I felt.

When I was sure no one could still see my face, I allowed the tears to slowly slide down. Though I generally smile and feel an immense amount of gratitude for my life, there are still certain occasions where I grieve what I have lost. Falling hard is one of those occasions. I grieve for what the stroke took from a physically fit twenty-seven-year-old body. I want you to understand being sad is okay, but it cannot become the main emotion to recovering, healing, and partaking in life in general. Tears slid down my face. Thankfully they were masked by my sunglasses. I dried them by the time I was home.

Within a few hours I was laughing again. Color already started showing on my derriere. I laughed at myself, thinking, "Wow, I never knew what it felt like to stop traffic before!" I smiled because I now had a great excuse to wrap up and sit on my warm and cozy heating blanket all day long. And again, I laughed because I still could, and it felt great.

I cried because I know it is okay to be sad. I laughed because joy has always healed me both physically and mentally. I laugh, I cry, and

I smile because having emotions is healthy and having optimism that always returns will help me overcome obstacles I may again, one day, be forced to face.

When Life Hands You Lemons

I am not going to say having seizures through my school years, losing the memories of having two children, or having a frontal temporal lobectomy followed by a stroke was an easy path to walk. I am not going to tell you that it did not cause periods of frustration and sadness. I will tell you though, after all is said and done, I am fortunate I was able to experience each of these trials.

Mrs. Bowman was an amazing teacher to the seventh grade students in Monticello. One of my favorite lessons I tucked away and carried with me was her explaining when life hands us lemons it is up to us to make lemonade. As with so many lessons throughout our schooling, they help prepare us in unexpected ways for life events that at the time are unpredictable. She did not give away a secret recipe. She only instilled in us that it can and will, with effort, be possible. It was up to us to make our own recipe. Just as she was unable to, I cannot give away a secret recipe. Thank you, Mrs. Bowman, for that lesson of life.

I can, however, confirm that it is possible. From my lemons, I have created the sweetest lemonade that has ever passed my lips. After my events, I decided I wanted a deeper understanding of the brain. I went back to school to become an electroencephalogram (EEG) technician. Due to a sudden move related to my husband's career, I had to drop out of the program. Before leaving, I gained the knowledge of what brain waves looked like and represented within our minds. I learned the very basics of our brain. After becoming settled in our new home, I still had this thirst for knowledge. I began applying to graduate schools and enrolled in a master's program for psychology. With the confidence that I gained in not only surviving but also thriving through previous obstacles, I rose to the challenge and applied myself fully to this program. Seven years after my stroke, I finished the program with a 4.0 grade point average. With this goal completed, I applied more focus to the education of my children than in the limitations set by my sight loss. After fighting against the school district budget cuts to reopen our elementary library, I became a librarian to help young students have access to the power of books and dreams.

No, my trials of frequent seizures, amnesia, a stroke, and sight loss were not easy challenges. Still, I would not give back a single day. All of these events – all of these lemons – have taken time to form and develop into something greater. I have peeled away the sour rind these events possessed. Now, I am squeezing the juices that are left behind from each lemon and enjoying the product of my struggles. The sweet lemonade offered to quench the questions of what will happen next and exposed the joy of unending awe and gratitude for everything I have left to enjoy.

Like I said, not a precise recipe for lemonade, but one anyone may follow. Embrace the challenges life gives us. Stand up to them and overcome the obstacles head-on. Do not shy away from challenges, but work hard and persistently at taking something positive away from each trial. Sit back, relax, and reflect on what opportunities life has given you. Take time to mourn if necessary. Take the needed period to experience regret, resentment and then take time to recover. Embrace with gratitude the unforeseen gifts you will find. Hopefully, you will see the challenge not as a burden but a lesson life has entrusted you with. Find what is positive within the experience. Figure out what it is you can take from this complication. Share the positive lesson that you will discover with your family, your friends, and society as a whole. The message you find needs to be shared. We can all learn from each other. After time, after healing and gaining insight into what may lie ahead for you, then relax. Sip your lemonade remembering your life is yours for the taking.

In seventh grade I sat behind the desk, like so many of my peers, staring with absent eyes listening to a teacher trying her best to shape the minds of her young pupils. I waited for the eternity it took for the bell to ring and hurriedly left the class. Twenty-some years later and I finally understand the message Mrs. Bowman was pushing into our minds. I wish I could go back and tell her today about the lemonade I have created. So sweet, even her creative writing lessons would leave me at a loss for the words to express the quench these lemons have found the power to produce.

Serving of Optimism: Opening Doors

I know a professor who often speaks of experiences he's had. These stories leave me entranced. The adventures fascinate everyone who has the opportunity to listen. He is from a smaller city yet has met some of the biggest names. I asked a person who knew him how he accomplished this. I asked how it was he connected with all of these people and has been invited to participate in monumental projects. She told me, "He answers his phone and the door any time someone calls or knocks."

This made me think. How often do I not answer the door, unsure of the strangers that may be there? How often do I let the phone go to voice mail because I may be too busy to answer? Maybe I need to be knocking on more doors. My dreams are there. My passion is there. Now I just need to make sure I am not waiting for others to open doors for me. There's no need to stare at the wall when I know the door is there waiting for me to open it. The knock is waiting for me to answer.

"Don't follow your dreams; chase them." Unknown

Finding Strength and Beauty From Within

I planted a gladiolus bulb over a year ago. I forgot about it. I had not even remembered Sandra brought the bulb last year as a gift for me. At that time, I planted it and watched it for a while. Then, sorry Sandra, I neglected to nurture it. An entire year went by before I remembered where it had been planted.

Maybe we all have a bulb similar to this within us. What do you think? I like to think deep inside us all, there is strength and beauty ready to blossom. This gladiolus bulb knew how to collect nutrients from the soil and conserve water from our scarce spring showers. Our nutrients are hope and joy.

There is a piece in all of us we don't take notice of or, in many cases, even remember. There is a strength and beauty ready to bloom which we too often forget to nurture. Under the right conditions, it will grow in all of us. Find your talent. Find a hobby that brings you joy. Find a way to make your tiny piece of the world better. Nurture it and watch the strength it possesses grow as it creates something special for all of those around you to see.

Take Time

I saw a car slow down in the parking lot of a nearby shopping center. It pulled up to a beautiful rose bush in full bloom. I watched a lady step out, walk up next to the bright apricot roses and bend over to smell the flowers. I looked to the opposite side of the lot and saw busy people walking fast and holding tight to full shopping bags. A line of cars was driving up and down aisles waiting for the nearest parking spaces to open up in a rush to get holiday gifts. As I turned back to the solitary woman, I saw she had pulled a camera from her car. She took pictures, zooming in and out towards the blooming flowers. As she lowered her camera to her side, she stepped forward again to take the opportunity to smell the roses.

There is a lesson for us all in her motions. As the old cliché goes, we should take time to stop and smell the roses. Many people feel they cannot take time with their busy schedules. Sadly, it often takes a life-altering event to understand the importance of this action. Take it from someone who has been given the opportunity to understand the importance and joy of taking time to cherish simple pleasures. It is worth taking a few seconds out of your busy schedule to smell the roses.

◡◞

A Secret Passage and Undiscovered Wildlife

*T*his summer I was fortunate to have created many new memories. I appreciate opportunities I have during the summer to take my children out of city living and expose them to treasures I found as a child in a rural area. We went camping one night during our summer trip. My daughters found a path which led to a creek bed behind where we were staying. Instantly there was a sparkle in their eyes as they noticed stepping stones that had become exposed by the drought. They felt certain no one else had a chance to see them because the water was usually too high. They were sure, beyond any doubt, this was a passage that had never before been discovered. In the innocent mind of children, they believed they were stepping into a space no one else had been lucky enough yet to find. This was their "secret passage". Now, I don't mean to ruin your imagination, but this was a common path many had taken before. Footsteps pushing into the grass on the other bank let me know someone had recently crossed this dried creek bed just as we were doing. Of course, I let their imaginations explode with possibilities. I let their excitement spread to me and we carried on up the bank to see where this secret passage may lead. Lucky for us, the magic continued….

We crossed this secret passage, climbed up a small hill, and there in front of us was a deer! My daughters had never discovered a deer on their own before. They saw one earlier that morning, but it had been a rescue animal confined in an enclosure while its wounds healed. Yet, this deer was alone in a nearby field. It became startled and ran away quickly. The secret passage led them to undiscovered wildlife! I have seen many deer throughout my life. I have seen them in fields, eating left-over food dropped by combines, and leaping too close to cars. Yet, I am still awed by their beauty and speed as they run from danger. I was grateful for the excitement and adoration this deer provided my daughters who had never seen one so close. Their awe was contagious as I again saw this animal's power and beauty as if for the first time.

My daughters gave me a gift that day. They reminded me to hold onto curiosity, excitement, and awe for things never before seen and also those which you were not expecting to see again so soon. My girls are old enough to know realistically someone had crossed the creek before them. Yet, they were able to use imagination and see a mystical adventure waiting for them to discover rather than an ordinary path. Can we all do this with our lives? Can you do it? Can you leave the house today and, rather than experience the boredom of yet another path you've gone on before, step out and explore what surrounds you as if it is yours alone to claim? Can you search with the eyes of a child and find new discoveries in an already-discovered world? My daughters allowed me to take a journey with them and to remember that, even though someone has seen something a thousand times, to others it is a remarkable sight they have never before seen.

Remember the discoveries that are made. Hold on to memories which are created. I hope you find an undiscovered passage that will offer you great joy and memories to cherish forever.

Critical Lesson for Medical Personnel

I am not so naïve as to believe that your medical background will not help heal me. However, there is a lot that you can learn venturing outside the classroom. There is a lot that you can learn from people like me. Come through my door. Come sit by my bed. Talk to me. Listen to me. There is so much that I/we, your patients, can help you learn…so much more than your college education can ever teach you.

Lessons: Truly, I am sorry that you may be having a bad day. I am sorry that your significant other snapped at you as you were leaving the house. I am sorry that your children were fighting at home this morning. Tonight I cannot see my kids. I have to stay here in this hospital bed. I really am sorry that life is giving you some problems right now; however, at this moment, I want to be your most important problem.

I know that you are concerned. I can see it in your eyes. I know that you care because you take a moment or two to really listen when you ask how I am feeling. The machines can continue beeping, but you cared because you took a moment to listen to me instead of to them.

I have had the opportunity to meet world-class medical personnel through my life experiences. Many were excellent providers of medical knowledge. Those names have slipped quietly away from my memory. A few, however, have been amazing providers of medical *care*. These people will forever remain in my mind. Dr. Howard: He cared not only about me, but about the care I received. I was not a scheduled surgery, I was a person (a wife, a mother, a daughter). Cheryl always asked about my children. She still has a smile that radiates the room when I stop by to say hi. Abby was an aide who brought me ice cream in a Styrofoam cup late one night to make me smile. We sat together and ate – most importantly, we smiled. Julie took time to shave my legs in the midst of her busy day. She did not have to, but I was eternally thankful. I may not have had any hair on my head but she still helped me feel feminine. Matt and Dana looked beyond the prognosis and into the hope I possessed. From this outlook, I have gained the ability to be the capable person I am today. Dr. Feinstein, Dr. Wright, and Dr. Duchaine all gave me time and support to find my weaknesses, allowing me to gain insight about my strengths. There are so many more. I do not remember their diplomas hanging from walls. I cannot tell you where most of them gained their education. Nonetheless, I can tell you what amazing hearts they possess. These individuals carried me when I did not have the strength to stand. I am grateful for the strength they helped me gain.

Yes, medical workers, please do bring your medical knowledge to my room. But it is your sincere care and consideration that will heal my soul. And only with my soul together again can I stand this tall. For that, you will never leave my memory. Thank you to every caretaker out there that knows that value of caring for the person, not just the patient.

Serving of Optimism: Glory Days

One good thing that comes from experiencing amnesia is you learn the true significance of embracing each memory and trying to cement it in your mind. I understand what Bruce Springsteen was singing about when he spoke of our glory days and how "they'll pass you by...in the wink of a young girl's eye." I not only lost my ability to recall glory days but all memories. My memories were gone, not in the wink of an eye, but through a rapid series of seizures. Now I savor each moment, understanding it may not be possible to hold in my mind the fleeing happiness and hope I fondly recall.

This past week was filled with memories I know I've captured as glory days. I was a guest in front of a live studio audience on the "Jeff Probst Show." I had special people visit from out of state. I had my daughters hold my hand and tell me I'm a great mommy. Little moments can easily pass us by. Oftentimes, we do not realize the importance of these moments until they are gone.

Tomorrow you may look back and realize the impact someone made on your life today. It often takes the passing of time to recognize positive changes and their origins. Someone else may look at the gift you gave them today, whether it was a simple smile or a kind word, and tomorrow – or days down the road – they'll remember what an amazing difference you made for them. They may not have the chance to tell you they still think of you fondly. Hold on to every gift of joy and happiness you experience. Someday, somewhere along the line you may look back and realize today was one of your many "Glory Days."

Right Where I Should Be

*T*his morning I left to go to the gym and noticed a white car driving away from our street. Before it reached the next stop sign, the brakes were applied; a woman jumped out from the driver's seat and started yelling, "Call 9-1-1! Someone call 9-1-1 quick!" She was screaming like a woman who suddenly had no control, only an intense fear. A girl jumped from the back seat and started running, knocking on doors. The lady continued screaming and crying out like an injured person. I heard her yell at the end of a breath, "My son is having a seizure." I reached the car as quickly as I could. Another adult was already looking into the vehicle. The boy in the car was twelve and just had a tonic-clonic seizure. He had never had medical problems before and was now unresponsive, which placed tremendous fear into this mother's heart. I asked the bystander to help the mother move the boy from a slumped position and lay him down on the seat. I explained her son was postictal. He was in the third phase of a seizure. I asked the other family member to speak to him with kind and calming words. I told the little boy an ambulance was coming to check on him, and I knew it probably seemed all really scary and confusing. I assured him everything was all over now and his body just needed to rest.

I told the mom again and again that resting like this after a seizure was normal. Her son was tired. This was the path to recovery. His brain and body were just relaxing now. The girl who had fled the back seat was his little sister. She had been the one to identify the onset of the seizure. She was scared and had no comprehension of what she had just seen. I asked if she had ever seen a lightning storm. We talked about rain when it sprinkles and then when it drops so hard you beg your mom to run outside and splash in the puddles. The little girl smiled as she heard about puddles. We discussed how it isn't a good idea to play in lightning. Her brother just had the coolest lightning storm that started in a little space in his brain and then spread all over. We talked about how cool it would be to see lightning spread like that. We talked about how cool it was he had a sister as great as her. She hugged me, wiped away tears, and hugged me again.

The paramedics came. I told them this little boy was postictal and the length of time since the movement stopped. We talked about his response of blinking a few times. It seemed as though he was coming to. I told his mom again and again how much harder this was on her than it was on her son. Before the ambulance drove away, the girl hugged me again and whispered, "Thank you."

A few hours later, I drove my daughters to listen to my youngest play in her second band concert. There is something beautiful, yet painful, about listening to fourth and fifth graders playing a mix of Queen songs. It kind of leaves me wishing I could not hear if instruments are out of tune. Yet, I can and I help my daughters practice their instruments. I am able to iron clothes and drive them to these performances. I've come a long way from only dreaming I could push down piano keys again.

I returned home to a neighbor waiting to share a glass of red wine and entertaining conversation. We had tears to clear up first. She found out today one of her eyes is losing sight and the eye doctor expects all sight to be gone within a short while. The other eye has macular degeneration and will progressively get worse over time. I told her about the neat devices I learned about while in a low-vision support group. I told her ways to cope that had helped me get around. When I first had my stroke, I was nearly blind. It was a slow process to get as much as I have back.

I told my neighbor one of the best lessons I learned: You don't have to see a picture to realize the beauty it holds. You don't have to see the sunset to recreate the splendor in your mind. We grieved the loss she will soon experience. Yes, there were tears. It's healthy to cry for what you are losing and to fear what might come. Yet, it is also healthy to hold onto hope and rejoice in what you still have. As I told her, when you lose a loved one, there are five stages of grieving. When you face a serious illness, these five stages are usually present and just as important. We lightened the mood and laughed at what amusing things it might be good *not* to have to see. I left after a big hug. As I walked home, I was slightly confused whether we still had tears of sadness or these were tears brought on by humor. Sometimes, as in this evening, they are so beautifully intertwined they are hard to differentiate.

Days like these once again reaffirm my belief that life does not prepare us for the current moment, but prepares us for moments yet to come. Someday you will find yourself understanding why the hard and trying lessons you learn today are so important for tomorrow. On this day, today, I found myself remembering this important lesson. I have no doubt; I am right where I should be.

CHALLENGES

*If life causes you to fall down ten times,
get back up eleven. Stand up to the challenge.*

The Evolution of Normal

I no longer think about what pictures I used to see in my mind. I know hearing words to remember an object is the only capability I have to "see" memories. I no longer rub my eyes and try to get the darkness created by hemianopia to disappear. My eyesight will always be missing on the left side. Until I wake up and pain shoots through my cramped muscles or a stranger asks what happened to my leg, it is no longer a conscious thought that I limp. The limitations I am left with are part of me. I am not defined by my disabilities. I am very aware they shaped me into the person I am today.

My past complications evolved me into the person I have been fortunate enough to become. I accept this as my new normal. Normal is a word we use to define what everyday life delivers to us. It is normal to research information on a computer. It is normal to travel by car. It is normal to see green grass in the spring and feel heat in the summer. Normal is acceptable. Normal is fairly consistent. Yet, never forget that normal will also evolve. What we thought was normal for us and for society ten years ago may not be considered our normal today.

When we sail along pleasantly through life and are struck by a painful or even life-altering event, the normal we are familiar with will be abruptly disrupted. This creates a troubled feeling. We usually don't enjoy being taken from our routine. These very routines define our perception of normalcy. I will tell you an important life lesson I learned. Normal will eventually come back to your life. It may not be exactly the same. Routines may change. You will probably change. Nonetheless, normal will return. You will adapt to your new normal as you gradually adapt to the changes in your life.

I hope your new, evolving normality will be accepted. It might be a hard adjustment. Give it time. I would like to read a magazine and not be confused by the content because I have missed seeing the left column. I would like my eyesight back. I would prefer not having to be concerned again if and when I would have another seizure – my Disease of Waiting. I want to feel various textures of clothing rubbing my left hand rather than only a rough, uncomfortable sensation as I fold clean clothes. I would like this a lot. Yet, I accept what I have now. I am grateful for the normal I have adjusted to experiencing. My senses from the past will not return. My normal is becoming a comfortable consistency I can now depend on. Remember yesterday but you cannot have it back. Tomorrow is unknown so do not worry too much about it. Today is a gift given just for you.

Yes, my normal has evolved. Yet, as my routines have changed, I am grateful for this new normal my life has delivered to me.

Serving of Optimism: Who We Can Become

Sometimes in life we are knocked down so far we may never think we'll be able to stand again. Sometimes in life we think we have forgotten who we are and begin to question who we may become. Never forget, life is a journey. Work hard. Enjoy every moment. And, most important, always leave what we pass by a little better than how we found it.

Being Disabled In an Able Body

*I*n an upcoming event I am scheduled to attend, I saw this option: "Individuals with disabilities are encouraged to attend all (school) sponsored events. Do you require an accommodation in order to participate in this program?" I thought a lot about this offer. Assistance would be nice. I do have disabilities. However, I think the organizers were thinking more along the lines of wheelchairs or assistance for low-sight individuals. My thoughts went more towards having people hold my hand and guide me in a world that sometimes leaves me a little confused.

If you pass by me, you will see a lady with a slight limp and a quick smile. You will see someone who sees where she is going but does not always see the hallway on the left she should've gone down when you said, "Take the first left." You will see someone who is grateful when you said you want to speak with her later, but she – having prosopagnosia – looks lost as she scans the room, suddenly panicked, noticing there are three men with graying hair wearing a navy jacket just like you. I am embarrassed when I leave a piece of my lunch hanging on my lip, but I don't know it is there because that area is still numb like the entire left half of my body was after my stroke. You cannot see any obvious physical hint showing my frustration when I look for the person who was going to walk me to the podium, but I fill with dread and worry when I don't see her as the room quickly fills with people.

I am a slightly disabled individual inside of, for the most part, an able body. I commented to someone how much I would appreciate if they would go with me to this particular event, so they could hold my hand. The comment was answered with a well-meaning chuckle saying they had no doubt I would be able to handle this on my own quite well. I hesitantly agreed. They were correct. I will do just fine on my own. I always do. But, believe me, sometimes facing a world you cannot fully see and being close to people you cannot recognize is more challenging than I may let on.

At the event I am attending, they want me to check an option if I "require an accommodation in order to participate in this program."

I will leave it unchecked. In one line, how do I explain I would like someone to come so I can hold their arm and have a friend to help guide me? There is no simple way to explain all of this within a small space, so I will eagerly seek out an individual who will understand when I say I am lost because I cannot recognize anyone in this room. Maybe they will be willing to walk around with me. Sometimes it is the invisible limitations that leave me so lost. Yet, I always try to remember, maybe it is these same limitations which have forced me to have grown so independent and so strong.

Climbing Mountains

I am thankful I discovered a new way to view mountains I encounter in life. Like many other people, I used to only see the trees and boulders blocking my way. I stood before the imposing sight and wondered how I, or anyone else, would ever have the strength to overcome this challenge. Now I realize on every mountain, hidden deep inside the rocky terrain, there is a smoother, less demanding path. Stand before your mountain. Look at the paths in front of you. Do not fear the intimidating height and overwhelming challenge. When you are nearing the top, reflect in awe over your accomplishments. You are conquering the mountain you once feared. At every plateau, take time to regain your balance. Smile and acknowledge the gratitude you feel from this accomplishment.

These mountains I've discovered have been both figurative and literal. I found myself waking up in a hospital bed, my body bruised and battered from the electrical attack seizures created in my brain. I celebrated my ten-year high school reunion not by playing the night away; instead, I was resting in a bed, partially paralyzed due to a stroke. Years later, I was 7,000 feet up the side of a mountain, armed with a strong stick to help me walk and a weak ankle wrapped in an air cast. I have come to realize fear and dread can develop into an overwhelming sense of hope and accomplishment. Climbing the path on these mountains is not easy. Finding strength to stand again is not simple. I have learned to accept it never will be. Self-confidence and joy found when you walk independently out of a hospital or gaze over the rugged terrain breathless and exhausted, observing the magnificent view, would never be experienced if not for the diligence to climb these mountains. Personal pride could never have been experienced if I were to have said, "This trial is too hard. Walk on without me."

While accepting the challenge of mountains, I have found great joy in discovering my own previously-unacknowledged strengths. I now challenge you to seek this benefit from difficult life experiences you were not expecting to encounter. On June 25, 2003, I went into pre-surgery at 5:15 a.m. I woke later that day unable to move half my body, displaying a smile that could only lift half my face. That day my journeys in life unexpectedly diverged. I knew I had a choice to make. I could lie there with the knowledge my life would forever be negatively changed and accept the grim outcome printed on so many fliers to inform me about stroke recovery. Or, I could accept that mountains sometimes come from unexpected events but can be overcome with hope developed from unfaltering optimism. Consciously making this choice would allow me to achieve progress that others would be compelled to write about – progress no one could have ever dreamed of – and defining hope that would inspire others around the world. Eight years later, I am still celebrating my choice of the latter.

Breaking through Doubt

I do not know of anyone who has ever achieved a milestone without first believing in themselves and acknowledging there is something special within them.

This past week was filled with practice after practice. There was a lot of extra time and effort spent in preparing for a test that meant a great deal to our daughters. This past week showed me, yet again, even though unpredicted obstacles may come our way, there is success if we have confidence that we can break through these obstacles.

Last weekend, my daughters had their first belt test in Tae Kwon Do. I now fully realize what my mom meant by saying it is harder to watch your kids compete than it is to compete yourself. Even though I knew they had the test memorized and practiced to near perfection, I could not help but worry they would miss a step or forget everything as fear engulfed them. I wanted them to taste success.

They met the challenge and achieved success. They did not doubt their abilities at all. Even when the boards were brought out to be broken, the girls did not flinch. This was the first time white belt students received instruction on how to break a board. My heart was racing and my hands were shaking. Both of my daughters looked the tester straight in the eye and did not seem fazed. I remain in awe of their self-confidence. They had no doubt the challenge could be overcome with a strong, fast fist and a slight, small kia (shout). In a child's eye, challenges can be overcome simply because they are there and, of course, you are supposed to break through challenges.

Maybe as adults we would do better if we kept this thought in our minds, also.

The Easter Bunny, Tooth Fairy, and a 5K

"If you do not believe, you will not receive." I grew up hearing these words. As we grow older, reality becomes our primary focus and our childhood dreams and imaginations fade away. When you are young, you do not question the joys you experience. You wake on a special day and find gifts left where you expected them. Your mystical imagination is rewarded. You continue to believe, without ever doubting, the Easter bunny will magically hide eggs and the Tooth Fairy will know you have lost a tooth. As you grow older, reality chips away at these fun and festive experiences.

My dreams and imagination are no longer centered on a loose tooth or hidden eggs; rather, I look at a pair of new running shoes and hold this same mystical fascination. I dream these may be the pair to carry me across a 5K race's finish line.

I had a stroke in 2003. I was twenty-seven. I spoke with a doctor shortly after waking up. It was then I learned I may never walk again independently. Because of those words, I promised myself I would work as hard as I could to once again walk alone. I was slow and cautious, but I walked by myself out the hospital doors. Now I walk at least three miles a day to keep up my strength and coordination. Yet, with all of this walking, I still am unable to run more than a block. I should be thrilled with a block I know. Yet, I want to continue pushing myself to regain the abilities the stroke stole from me. The muscle groups no longer work together to allow me to run, but I work hard to try, regardless. Whether I make it two strides or two driveways, I constantly work to reach this next milestone. I still dream of what others claim is no longer a reality.

Realistically, new shoes will not allow me to run the 3.1 miles I dream of. New shoes will not offer the security I will never fall again. They will not prevent my toe from dropping, causing it to catch and me to fall. Yet, I like to dream the chance of running a 5K is a reality. I like to make-believe the Easter bunny will be dropping off a basket of exquisite dark chocolates in a fun Easter basket. I hope the Tooth Fairy will not oversleep next time my little ones lose a molar. There is something fun, hopeful, and exciting when we allow ourselves to suspend our disbelief and cherish our dreams. Dreams, sometimes unrealistic, can once again be real...even if only within the magic of our imaginations.

From the Couch to Dreaming of a 5K

It generally holds true that we always want what we cannot have. You may have never heard of the over-priced product before you saw the ad. Now you need it. You had something in your possession for a year and never touched it. You only recognized its value after giving it away. Never before was I a runner. Never before did I want fancy, high-heeled shoes with straps running up my legs. My strong desire of wanting what I cannot have is noticed more often now than ever before.

I walk through a mall and look starry-eyed at those pretty shoes. What I would not give to wear those out of that store. I talk to local friends, read social media posts, and am awed at how many of my acquaintances are training for short runs and marathons. I am so impressed with all of you that have the motivation to get off the couch and take that run. Now that I cannot join you, I want to more than ever. Everything has changed.

My body denies me this ability. I used to have the leg coordination to walk in whatever shoes I wanted to. Before, I never cared whether or not my shoes were fashionable. My legs used to be healthy enough to run as far as my lazy motivation would encourage me to go. I used to take these gifts for granted. Now the lingering effects of a stroke have taken these abilities from me.

My body has been robbed of the ability to do these seemingly simple things. According to physicians, I will never again be able to run any extended distance. I usually make it about a block before I stumble and fall. What I would give to get back those healthy legs. I would run ten marathons and walk home from each of them in my fancy, high-heeled shoes!

Yet, in losing these abilities, I have gained a much different, but just as harbored, treasure. I no longer have the physical ability to run, but I walk and I can share my story with others. Enjoy the body you have, and utilize all the gifts that you have been given! Four years post-stroke I completed a walk of four miles. That might not seem like very far to some, but to me it felt as if I had broken the tape ending the Boston Marathon. I crossed that finish line with my daughters by my side. We raised our arms in triumphant joy. We celebrated all day. The next day, I sent out a flyer declaring "Four Years – Four Miles." No, I did not finish that marathon I long for, but I climbed to the top of my mountain that day. A mountain, four years prior, that seemed too steep to ever dream of conquering.

Yes, I deeply treasure the fact that I can still walk. Nevertheless, I hold tight onto the dream that one day again I may be able to run. I wake some mornings having filled the night with dreams that I am running once again. I imagine that I am running through a field of tall grass and wildflowers swaying along my swift legs. Do not be saddened by this repressed dream that comes to life only in my sleep. I am happy to hold on to the hope of "maybe someday." I am also thrilled with how far I have come from roaming the hospital halls in a wheelchair.

Do not be sad, but please do one thing for me. If you are out today, run down the block. Please, just one block for me. Recognize what it feels like when the wind pushes against your face. Feel the pull in your legs. Hold onto the pressure in your chest as your body begins to work harder. I dare you to even push yourself for a solid two blocks. Let me know how it feels, good or bad. You are so lucky that your legs still work that well. Hold onto the amazing qualities that your body has. Do not take the simple things for granted. Tomorrow you may look back with longing, wishing that you could have done something that you never took time or effort to try and long for what you can suddenly no longer obtain. And, my friends preparing for your next big race – know that when you are getting really tired and ready to call it quits, I think you are amazing for pushing your abilities so far. Thank you for sharing your motivating stories with me!

A View of My World

Take a picture of a busy street. Place a black sheet of paper over the left half of your photo. This is what I see as I look down the same busy street. I have left homonymous hemianopia. As a result of my stroke, the left half of my sight is now always completely black. I have no ability to see the left half of the visual fields from either my right or left eye. I am lucky the remaining eyesight, straight forward and to the right, have remained normal.

Another way to explain homonymous hemianopia is using the example of an analog clock. When I look straight at its center, I will see the digit 2 in the 12 on top. The digit 1 is completely black as are 7, 8, 9, 10, and 11. I am able to clearly see the other 1, the 2, 3, 4, 5 and part of the 6. If I look directly at someone's nose, I can see their nose and the left half of their face. If I look at their left ear, the face will disappear into darkness. Please understand my missing eyesight is not what causes prosopagnosia. Rather, that stems from a different area in the brain. Even if I regained my ability to have a complete, unhampered view of the world, I would still not be able to remember a face again.

Having complete or homonymous hemianopia is different from losing sight from one eye since the sight remaining from the good eye still allows for some peripheral capability. The unaffected eye will normally have the complete ability to see side views to assist with deficits created by the affected eye. Lacking peripheral sight on one side from both eyes can be extremely challenging.

So how does this lack of eyesight alter my daily living? I walk into walls I do not notice. I find it difficult to determine if someone is talking to me because it is challenging to see where their eyes are directed. Shaving is more difficult when half of the leg disappears. Vacuuming is an unending chore: I think I have cleaned the entire room only to turn my head and realize there was a large section I did not see. Cooking is also negatively affected. This is most noticeable when I am using a knife. When my left hand holds a vegetable, my right hand will cut. While looking at my right hand and where the knife is coming down, I will not be able to see my left fingers. It becomes dangerously easy to cut myself. Also, there is a major decrease in depth perception, especially as night falls. Reading has also taken on unexpected challenges. When reading articles in magazines, I am often confused trying to follow the story. I easily miss the columns on the left.

Yes, with missing eyesight, a whole new array of challenges presents itself. Learning to compensate was one of the great gifts created because the majority of my eyesight was missing when I awoke after my stroke. At first, most of my world was black. It was a very gradual process to regain the sight I now have. When possibilities of what I could regain were first discussed with my physicians, we did not know what would be recovered. I had doubts my sight would ever improve. Essentially I could have been blind for the rest of my life and never have seen my daughters' faces again. By the time I could see fifty percent from each eye, I was extremely relieved. I went from waking up to a dark room to being able to notice small details in faces and photos. I had the ability to get around without any added assistance. With the sight I now have, I was able to reclaim an independent life.

I hope you have noticed that nowhere in this article is the word "vision" used when explaining what I have lost. There is a definite difference between how these two words can be defined. Initially, I lost a lot of my eyesight. Currently, I still have a substantial portion of my eyesight missing. I would love to no longer walk into walls or hit my head on open cabinet doors. A large amount of my sight is gone and will probably, realistically, never return. Yet, I have not lost my vision. If anything, at the time my sight disappeared, my vision for life became even clearer. I carry hope and happiness daily in every aspect of my life. I have a vision to share this hope with everyone I can get my message to as I speak of being a young stroke patient, living with epilepsy and prosopagnosia. I no longer have sight, but I am filled with a tremendously powerful vision!

Prosopagnosia and Sight Loss: Visions and Dreams

Two questions always asked when I am speaking to people about my limitations are: "When you have lost so much vision, how hard is it for you to cope?" The other: "Since you have lost most of your visual memory and ability to recognize faces, do you still have dreams?"

Now, I am fully aware what is being asked, "Does it bother you that you can't see as well as you used to?" and "What fills your mind at night?". I know these are their questions, but I hope the real meaning is never misunderstood by people I am trying to educate and inspire. My answers in short: Yes, I would like to see more. Yes, I still have thoughts that fill my sleep but not images.

The longer answers: In the previous article "A View of My World," I explained how you can create a picture which helps demonstrate the way I see the world with left homonymous hemianopia. I do have a lot of sight missing, but vision is not always a definition of what you see in front of you. I have goals for my future. I have a plan designed to guide me towards achieving great things. I am not lacking vision.

Dreams are not always the images and pictures your imagination creates. Sometimes a dream is what you hope for in the future. I do have hope. Regarding the night dreams people are referring to when asking this question, my imagination still fills my sleep with stories at night. The stroke took away more than my ability to remember a face. It also took away my visual memory which encompasses more than faces. Now my dreams are limited but still very realistic. I no longer see pictures of people running. I no longer see the cliff I am stepping off, but I still wake with a falling sensation. I still have dreams that leave me uneasy in the morning or can cause tears to come in the night. As in my waking hours, no images fill my mind. With closed eyes, I experience only darkness. My dreams are remembered in a mind that no longer sees pictures.

Have you ever read a really good book? A book so good you could not turn the pages fast enough? This book had you full of anticipation, and you refused to put it down until you finished the last page. Have you ever read a book that caused tears to stream down your face? This book may have left you stressed and saddened for the rest of the day. These are similar to my dreams at night. I do not see images, but I understand the occurrence through the words I think and sounds I hear.

How does someone without visual memory and prosopagnosia dream so vividly at night? Here is an example of a nightmare that haunted me: I remember singing with my two children in the car. (I could hear the wind blowing fast and felt movement. My daughters were asking if we were going to be there soon.) I screamed as the shattering glass sliced my skin open. (I could hear the screeching of brakes quickly followed by the sounds of metal scratching. I knew there was pain. The song my children sang was replaced by haunting screams and sounds of horror and pain.) The ambulance came and first took away my children, leaving me behind. (I heard the sirens. Someone was telling me to stay calm. My girls' voices were becoming fainter as they cried out "Mommy" and said they did not want to have to go without me.) I woke after that. I had no memory of seeing anything. Regardless, I did not need images to get me out of bed to go check on my children. I did not need pictures to feel the pain and fear that lingered throughout the day. As an avid reader, I have always known that words can be just as powerful, if not more, as watching pictures pass across a screen.

I do not need sight to have a vision. I have enough words, memories, and hope to always have dreams. Yes, prosopagnosia and hemianopia have certainly altered the way I see and feel, but I believe I have gained more and understand more now. This outweighs all I have ever lost. I love the vision and dreams that promise an exciting future.

Game On

While I was walking, I came up alongside two women. I could not help but overhear their conversation. One was talking about how horrible it was when she was visiting someone's home and they reorganized the dishes after she had worked hard to put them away. The homeowner, having had her dishes put away, said thank you but then went right back to moving around the plates! Terrible! A tragedy! How RUDE! Her voice was getting louder and higher as she related this horrific tale. Her friend could not help but give in and agree how rude this was. She even suggested that her friend might not want to go over to visit this house again for a while.

I often have trouble relating to moms in the area where we now live. Their frustrating issues in life, while horrible for them, seem so minor in my eyes. When I had my daughters in volleyball, the usual Thursday practice conversation revolved around how irritating it was that grandparents, sisters, or other family members would not be willing to watch kids for the weekend when these moms wanted to get out of the house. Once, I cautiously threw in that they were lucky to have family close. My family all lives 1,800 miles away. They scrunched up their noses and said how terrible it was we had no one around to "take our kids out of our hair." I laughed. It was not that long ago I did not have hair. It had been shaved off for brain surgery. I bit my tongue. I did not think there would be anything gained adding this to their conversation.

I am not attempting to minimize the problems other people face, but I do wish they would look at the bigger picture of life. Someone else always has it worse. I know there are plenty of people who have had greater struggles in life than those I endured. My stroke altered my life, yet there was never a chance it would end it. So, what was it like to have a stroke in my twenties? It was not fun. It is not an event I would recommend, but I did learn my true strength at that time. Thankfully, I did not have to experience defeat. Life tried, but I won. But in winning, I had a label placed on me by some – "Disabled." I cringe when I hear that word. I am too busy being "able" to ever pay attention to the first part of this title.

The lady who had the clean dishes reorganized was very agitated that her hard work was redone. I was agitated when my toe caught and I fell down yet again, the second time on a walk. I did not feel anger or frustration. After all, eight years ago, I could not go for a walk longer than between hospital doorways. Maybe the volleyball moms were truly angry when family members would not drop what they were doing to watch their kids. I am thankful I can see my kids play at a park and hear them laughing on a lazy Friday afternoon. I try to always remember there are people out there who cannot walk. I know of people who do not have families to safely go home to. Everyone can find a silver lining. In life, each of us will find individuals better or worse off than we are in that moment. Life is not easy. Life is not really supposed to be. Accept challenges that demonstrate your strengths.

Every person has been filled with frustration and disappointment at one time or another in their lives. We have all faced challenges at one point. Some of you are currently facing overwhelming worries. Just remember this. Maybe someone has hurt your feelings. Maybe your children are not creating the calmness you desire. Yet, you woke up today. You are breathing. You are seeing the light of a new day. Challenges will test us, but we have the strength to rise above them. Be stronger, be greater, and be more hopeful than yesterday. Put your feet on the floor. Grin as you tell the world, "Game on." Then go conquer the challenges that await.

Opening the Door for Opportunities

I answered a proverbial knock at my door that I was nearly too intimidated to answer. I was given an invitation to travel and speak to a college class. While this idea excited me and offered a chance to provide education on various topics I am passionate about, it also filled me with doubt and fear. I was traveling eighteen hundred miles (about 2,900 kilometers) to present to a group of students who had life experiences I could never guess and who knew nothing of the challenges I faced. Could we connect? Could I provide them the chance to gain as much as I would receive from this opportunity?

I heard a knock at the door and nearly let this opportunity pass by. While my message is important and I know nearly everyone can take something away from what I share, I did not know whether my message was worthy of this type of invitation. Then words of wisdom were shared with me, "You would not have been asked if they did not think you were good enough to provide their class with an enriching message."

I took a deep breath and answered the door. Here is the introduction the Life Design class saw on their Facebook page regarding my visit:

> "Tuesday's guest to class is a very special woman, Tara Fall. Tara suffers from a condition known as prosopagnosia, or "face-blindness." While her story is certainly about overcoming adversity, it is also an empowering tale of the lessons learned along the way. If you'd like a sneak peak, please…"

Now it's time to board a flight and explore the opportunities waiting for me. If my goal is achieved I will, in the words of the class's professor, "make the audience laugh, make them cry, but most importantly make them walk away thinking." I am truly grateful and excited I've opened the door. I encourage you to answer the knock on your own door. When the opportunity knocks, take hold of it. Do not let fear stand in your way. *Carpe articulum…*Seize the moment!

The Partially-Blind Librarian

In late 2007, the library at the elementary school my children attended was closed due to district budget cuts. For a year I fought, begged, pleaded, and fought some more to have the doors reopened. I succeeded. Amazingly though, this came with me being selected as the new librarian. It did not seem possible. I have prosopagnosia. I cannot recognize a face even if I see it on a daily basis. I only knew the teachers' names because of their rigidly-assigned class time to be in the library. The students I only knew because of the library cards they would hand me with their names written on them. With hemianopia, my world is always half black. I have lost my left peripheral sight. During story time, kids would giggle as I skipped part of their story. They always thought I was teasing to see if they were paying attention. They never realized I was only confused because, for me, a section of the story was visually missing. When part of your sight has been completely lost, it can make reading a challenge at times. But I knew those books and the chance for the kids to sit and read again were more important than any trials that may evolve. I fought hard for those kids. I worked hard to get the books ready for their anxious hands and inquisitive eyes. The library, as limited as it might have been, turned out to be a great success.

We were selected by an amazing program which awarded our school with a complete library makeover. They fulfilled my dream. The kids suddenly had the opportunity to sit in new, comfortable chairs. They had an array of new, hot-off-the-press books they were eager to read. Every child had a place in which they could store their dreams and allow their imaginations to run wild. This makeover allowed me to complete this dream and offer the kids all of this. I, a person who could neither recognize a face nor have the ability to spontaneously see many written words, got ready to see the ribbon cut to a room that had been void of voices, void of lights, and holding only untouched books before I fought for it.

My final lesson for the library, before my family had to move from the area, was a simple one. I explained to the kids that the child in the wheelchair may have a limited physical body, but their mind can be fascinating. That the deaf person who talks only with their hands still has amazing things to say – you just have to learn to listen a little differently. And a librarian that may use a white-tipped cane to find her way around a busy airport might not have sight but still can possess a powerful vision. Now, because I did not give up and fought for what I believed in, all these kids I cared so deeply about prepared to enter into a new world only limited by where their imagination will carry them. They now see the full meaning of my last lesson: Look at my ability. Do not judge me by my disability. A vision is very powerful.

Thank you to everyone who rallies for causes which will make others stronger and better. By doing so, many dreams have the chance to come true!

⌒⌒⌒

Ball Cap, Dark Sunglasses, and Defense Mechanisms

*A*ccording to Merriam-Webster, a defense mechanism is defined as "an often unconscious mental process (as repression) that makes possible compromise solutions to personal problems." Defense mechanisms are not thought about or planned, rather something that develops as a spontaneous reaction. I have become quite skilled at this. Recently I noticed I had developed a new defense mechanism – wearing a ball cap and dark sunglasses.

Not long ago, I went on vacation back to my hometown. I was concerned about how I would respond when "familiar strangers" approached me to pick up conversations we left off having years ago. I knew people would remember me. They would remember what we used to discuss or anecdotes regarding when we last saw each other. My reaction to these people would be a mixture of confusion and quietness. This reaction could be viewed as a lack of interest. This, however, is very far from the truth.

Having acquired prosopagnosia, or face blindness, does not necessarily mean a person who used to be very social is destined to become shy and inverted. The need for social interaction – the desire – is still there for me. I still want people to visit with me. I am still excited to catch up with old friends and be introduced to strangers. There is an awkwardness that comes from being in a place where you were outgoing before prosopagnosia altered your life, leaving you now unable to identify familiar people by facial recognition. Prosopagnosia, similar to epilepsy and the sight problem I have developed, is not noticeable to others that see me pass by them.

According to the way they view me, I am still just a local girl who moved away for an extended time.

And so, the awkward moments are inevitable. I become shy and unsure of myself when I know people will notice and remember me. I struggle with a way to tell people who have known me for twenty years that I no longer have a clue who they are. Anyone who has ever spent time in a small town understands when I say "everyone knows everyone." They notice when a new person walks around town. They also notice when natives come back to visit family. People noticed me.

I went back to this small town with questions and concerns filling my mind. How do I explain to people that I still think highly of them, that I continue to carry great memories of them, but I apologize for having no clue who they are. How do I tell people my memory of their faces is completely gone, but the memory of occurrences still remains strong? How do I not confuse people who just wanted to say "hello" and "welcome back"? How do I get close to familiar people when I can only see strangers? I had more questions than answers. Because of these lingering questions and concerns, I developed my most recent defense mechanism.

Several people came up to me at church and said they were surprised I was back in town. They questioned how I was and how long I would be back. I did not mind these questions. It was a comfortable environment. I remembered everyone at our small church and knew who usually congregated with whom. Some people even sat in the exact same spot they have for years! I grinned as they asked these questions, delighted to see old friends. One person said, "Are you back with your kids? We could not help but wonder if that was you!" They explained they did not want to holler out because they were unsure who the new person in town was. How did I not get recognized when everyone else can recognize others easily?

Every time, before I stepped out of my parents' house, I made sure I grabbed a few important things. I always slipped on some dark sunglasses. I pulled a ball cap tightly down over my forehead. I did not think about how I never used glasses and a cap back at my own home. I did not consider how different I appeared when no one could see my face. Yet, I did use an unconscious mental process to solve my personal problems. I found a way to reverse how people would know me now. I found a way to allow myself to become the familiar stranger walking quietly along my hometown sidewalks.

Fortunate Teachers can Still be Taught

With this amazing adventure I have been on, I have the ability to touch people's lives. This is not something I take lightly. I write messages for thousands of people to read. I have been on national television and have spoken to international media. Whenever I have a request to talk to a group, I make every possible effort to go and explain the lessons life has taught me. It has been an amazingly rewarding adventure to find that something positive is coming from what could initially have been perceived as a very negative experience. Yet, not surprisingly, the most rewarding part of my journey is not what I have been given but what I have the opportunity to give.

Fortunate teachers can still be taught. I have reached out to researchers around the world and have volunteered countless hours of my time. I want these brilliant minds to learn as much as possible from the medical complications I have survived. I must admit my goals are not entirely altruistic. You see, for everything they learn from me, I learn just as much from them. I hear lessons in their questions and gain knowledge from their results.

My children look to me for guidance. At a very early age, I learned my two beautiful girls would be able to teach me lessons about life as I placed my effort in teaching them. Through them I have truly gained comprehension in lessons of forgiveness, immense kindness, and unconditional love and trust. I have taught them, but unexpectedly they have also taught me very important life lessons.

Too often situations are rushed into. Voices are raised and assumptions are made. Yet, isn't it possible those we go to instruct can teach us? A coworker who seems to not understand the project may have a different way to reach the end result that is not so complicated. A patient that goes to his doctor may be able to reveal more than the test results can show. Sometimes we need to step back from the role of the instructor. In silence, we may be able to learn from what is going on around us in our busy lives.

I want to teach others what it is like to have hemianopia and no longer have peripheral eyesight. I hope to spread an understanding of what prosopagnosia means and how it can alter a life. My story is of being a young stroke patient and will educate individuals that anyone can have a stroke. I am eager for my experiences to provide hope that having a seizure disorder may slow you down but will be powerless to stop you from creating and achieving goals. I am always eager to find the comments offered to my blog posts. In lectures, I grow increasingly excited as we work towards the question and answer session. I know by statements left behind and questions being explored, I can gain knowledge of what others think, feel, see, and understand. I can grow from the stories people hold within their minds.

Because of this, I want to know your story. How has the world altered you? How are you using your gifts to touch the world and make a positive difference? I am a teacher, but more than this I am still thirsty to be a student and gain knowledge. I want to learn from the lessons your life has taught you. Everyone is important. Everyone has a story.

⌒

Military Dependents Can Find Independence

I was twenty-two when I married my husband. I had no doubt at that age I could single-handedly take on the world. I think being fearless at younger ages allows us to grow, explore, and unleash our abundant energy. The idea of marrying and moving hundreds of miles from my family, only to then – within a few months – move again over a thousand miles, seemed an easy accomplishment. With this pleasant ignorance, I did not see there would be any trouble going from a small town to big cities far away.

Within a short time, I had an eye-opening understanding that it's not easy to be an adult. Suddenly I had a different last name, a different state's driver's license, and I was labeled as a dependent. That word alone bothered me at age twenty-two! I was now a dependent to a Navy Petty Officer, and I was a little scared of this big, new world. In learning what it meant to be a "dependent," I also discovered a lot of incredible opportunities were waiting for me. I had amazing adventures at the first duty station. I learned that family is sometimes more than just the group you are born into. Family can also be defined by the support system you choose to develop. I realized it is okay to fall down as long as you gather the strength to stand again. I discovered it is easier to get back on your feet when you keep reliable friends nearby. The friends I first met so long ago remain close to my heart today, years later. Most importantly, I learned that being a "dependent" is not a label of weakness but one that defines strength and teaches the true lesson of how to become independent.

The next memorable time I thrived as a dependent was in 2006. I had my epilepsy surgery a few years before that. I recovered well from the stroke I experienced during this surgery. The Navy had allowed my husband to focus on his family before his work. This priority shift was needed and never forgotten. I continue to be awed at how well the Navy family takes care of our family. At that time, I was still carefully watched over by my friends, my family, and my community. It was time to step out of the community I had become used to relying on. It was time to discover my full potential that was waiting for me in my recovery. In order to do that, I needed to once again fulfill the role of a true, strong, military dependent. Early in 2006, we again moved half-way across the country to California. My husband immediately became attached to a ship. He left on a deployment for eight months. I recovered enough to once again succeed in the roles of a stay-at-home mom, mentoring newer military wives, and rediscovering the strength I knew I had. In reestablishing my role as a Navy dependent far from home again, I was able to reach my full potential for independence.

As my nation celebrates July 4th, I will also be celebrating my own independence. I am grateful to all the people, past and present, who have placed themselves in harm's way to keep our nation free. This freedom allows me the ability to not worry about countless subjects so many people take for granted as I celebrate the many gifts that come with being an American. I continue to be grateful that this independence allowed me to marry a service member and find my own place in our military's community. I will celebrate as I thrive in the role of being a dependent part of my family.

Benefits to Pain

People often ask, "Why do I have to hurt like this? Why do I need to be in such pain?" The pain being referred to is sometimes a mental anguish. Other times the pain being resisted is of a physical form. Either way, these are common questions. To feel no pain is a normal, understandable wish. From my life lessons, I offer this warning: Be careful what you wish for!

At one time, I certainly had the same sentiment. This resistance to pain would commonly be a blessing for many. Following my stroke, I had that very ability. On my left side, I could feel no pain. This actually became more of a curse than a blessing. I burnt myself one day in the kitchen. I thought I was feeling something very cold like my countertop, yet my finger was lying against a hot skillet. I can only tell if I am over-exercising by the pull and strain I feel on the right side of my body. I would not be aware if I pulled a muscle in my left leg or arm. Once, I had to have x-rays of my ankle. The doctor could tell I was limping more. I knew something did not seem right. Yet, even if my ankle had broken after I fell off a sidewalk, this would not have felt obvious to me. Another experience led to my losing a toe nail. The doctor asked if I had kicked my toes against something hard or if I dropped an object on my foot. I was clueless as to what trauma occurred causing enough damage for the toe nail to discolor and then fall off. I did not have the ability to feel any pain, even intense pain, which would cause such a significant problem.

I know what it is like to hurt. I know what it is like to wish the pain could just disappear. I also know that sometimes feeling no pain is just as challenging as feeling pain so severe you believe you cannot take any more suffering. Trust me as I tell my story: It is sometimes better to feel as if the hurt will cause your body to break than to have your body break and never know the damage and brokenness were ever occurring.

⌒

Finding Peace in My Broken Pieces

I enjoy a good jigsaw puzzle. I like to open a brand new box, shake the pieces out, and let my eyes roam over what the creation will be once it is all properly put together. I always start by finding the four corner pieces. Isn't that what we were always taught? Start by finding the four pieces that will make the strong edges – everything else will later depend on these. Day by day, slowly, piece by piece, you can take the jagged edges and find a way to gently place them together. The work can progress slowly, or you can go fast. Either way, once you have created a connection, brought life back to one complete project instead of a mismatch of disconnected pieces, you will be amazed at the brilliant picture you have created.

I like to think that is how we all are. Deep within us, aren't we all like the shattered jigsaw puzzle stored in the box? You can find examples in your soul, your spirit, and even your body. At one point, we are all beautifully complete. Yet, within a moment, our blissful world can shatter, leaving us physically or mentally in pieces. But, never forget what the untouched image had, at one time, looked like. It was a beautiful accumulation of pieces. In putting ourselves back together, we have time to examine all the individual aspects in our lives. Once we have taken the pieces, one by one, to slowly recreate the original image, we find out so much about ourselves. When we are once again whole, the image we come to know can be spectacular. This completed image can provide us with a peace that our fast-paced lives often cause us to forget.

Whether it is a surprising blow, a long drawn out painful situation, or something you thought might happen yet never truly expected, take a moment and let yourself be surrounded by these shattered pieces of your life. Then recreate the wonderful image you can build again. Fit your pieces together and become stronger as you realize what treasures your body and mind truly hold. Fall down, shatter, and I hope someday you will learn the important lesson in life I have discovered time and time again: Within my broken pieces, I can find peace.

Hitting My Head on Glass Ceilings

I have two young daughters. Every possible opportunity I have, I tell them the career options open to them are limitless. If they want to be a nurse or a teacher, that is possible. If they want to be a doctor or a fighter pilot, they can do it. I will help them work hard to achieve their dream of flying to the moon if that is what they want to spend their lives doing. I tell them they are lucky to be living in a world where the only thing which will hamper their accomplishments is their own drive. If they work really hard in school and in life, they can be anything they want to be when they grow up! Yet, I feel kind of silly saying these words. I feel slightly dishonest in what is generally a very honest relationship. Does it really matter how hard you work in the long run? I know, unfortunately, some things will hold you back regardless of how much effort you apply in your life. I know I have hit my head often on the ceilings made of glass that other people may have trouble seeing.

My dream job? When I grow up, I would love to be an EEG technician. Those are the people who play with glue and stick electrodes to patients' heads to record and monitor brain waves. I have been the recipient of many EEGs. I even went to school for this line of work. However, after a year into this two-year program, Uncle Sam called my husband (and therefore my family) and told him he had two weeks to leave Iowa and report to Naval Station San Diego. I gave up that career dream. I packed our bags. We moved together as a family.

This was my second time attempting this line of work. The first time was when I was seventeen and just starting college. Reality hit hard and quick. I realized it would be unrealistic to apply to this particular program. I had epilepsy at that time. How could I use a strobe light to induce seizures in clients when it would cause me to seize right alongside them? I knew better. I picked psychology instead. With years of holding onto the dream of being an EEG tech, I was extremely excited to actually begin the program some ten years later free of the complications my own seizures had provided. The sky was the limit.

Since ending the EEG program, I have been known to quietly blame my husband's job, but in retrospect I think it was for the best. I have learned a lot about myself and the current conditions I have been left with. I have greater understanding of my limitations than I had when attending school. What I am certain of is that I had a tremendous amount of trouble finding a distinction between the different brain waves. Now I understand why. My visual memory is lacking. I probably would never have been able to decipher what was an alpha wave and what was a theta wave. Sure, I can recognize the difference when I have a chart beside me, but identifying and naming these waves as they are displayed quickly on a screen would probably have been beyond my abilities regardless of how hard I tried to memorize the information. I was great at measuring and placing electrodes. I was terrific with offering patients support and information, yet the most important part of the job never would have been obtainable even if I had been granted the opportunity to complete the program.

And so the search continues. What is it that I want to be when I grow up? Right now I am a full-time mom, author, and speaker, but what happens when the mom role is no longer needed so extensively? A teacher would be a difficult role. I currently help in classrooms but refuse to go on field trips due to prosopagnosia (a.k.a. face blindness).

I would not be able to recognize which children were my responsibility getting onto the bus or roaming through museums. I have trouble with working in a store when customers' appearances cannot be recalled. I have a realistic fear that I may not drive much longer. How do I commute to work? How can I find someone to pick me up each day? We have moved into a community with very limited public transportation. Someday I will find a dream job that fits just for me. Thankfully, I am not grown up yet. I still have quite some time to think about what I want to do when I am all grown up. Until then, I am lucky enough to spend every day being the best mom possible for my children!

I chose to write on this subject to gently remind people that glass ceilings exist in different forms. They are not simply bound to gender. Now they are more specific to individuals. If you do have a job applicant with a disability, take a second look at their file before you pass over it. Usually if an individual has a limitation and is seeking employment regardless of their difficulties, that individual is hopeful and hard-working. They overcame a great deal to be where they are. I wish everyone could see the problem-solving abilities that are never taught in books but learned only through experiences a life involving limitations can provide. Help remove the glass ceilings and remember to open the doors for the abilities a disabled person has to offer.

Cherish Your Memories

*M*emories. Cherish Them.
Hold Them As If They Will Last Forever.

Each of us holds memories that are unique to us alone. These memories are glimpses into our past and offer hope and guidance for our future. Memories. Cherish them. Hold on to them as if they could last forever. Unfortunately, some people lose their memories. A condition known as amnesia can wipe away memories from a day, a few months, or even a lifetime. In more drastic cases, surgeons have to remove a section of the brain that holds a patient's memories. Cherish the memories that you have.

There was a man who had just turned fifty-six. He was an amazing craftsman with wood. From a tree, he could make nearly anything. This had been his hobby and later his livelihood. One day he woke up with no recollection of his past. Early in therapy he was handed a piece of wood. He slowly, cautiously, picked it up after staring at it for a while. He lifted it to test its weight. He rubbed his hand over it to feel its texture. He was startled when he received a splinter. This man had lost all memories of the look and feel of wood. He had spent his entire life building a career that was no longer possible to continue. If you have no memories of the past, on what do you base your future? How do you continue and create new memories? Imagine working your entire life to become successful in a field and then waking to have no recollection of the job you did. How do you earn a living? How do you make a new life? Cherish your memories.

I have often heard ladies say they wished they could forget about the delivery stage of pregnancy. I have heard many more say that pregnancy was not too bad until those last few weeks. If they could just erase those memories and the delivery, too…that would be so nice. I have even heard men say they wished they could erase the delivery images from their mind. Yuck! They did not need to see their wife's body do that! But, what if you would lose that memory? What if you would not remember the birth of your children? If they brought kids into your room and told you that you had them, but you never remembered being pregnant, how does that change who you are as a mother? As a human, to have a large milestone such as this wiped from your memory, how does that change who we are? Cherish the memories – even the memories that are painful, even the ones that are not pleasant. Hold on to them as if you would never let them go.

In more drastic cases, a surgeon needs to remove the memory section of a brain. There is a documented case of a young violinist. She was a child prodigy. She played at concert halls making amazing music until the surgeons called her parents in for test results. They had found a tumor. It was located over what appeared to be the memory section holding music. They would need to remove that portion of her brain. Without any other options, they sent this brave little girl into surgery. The surgery was successful. She was sent home to recover. One day, she asked her dad to bring in her violin. He said no. He tried to explain that she was not yet strong enough. In truth, he could not bear to explain to this young child that her memory of music was gone and she would no longer have the ability to perform the music she had once played. Whether she loved it or loathed it, she had practiced hours each day, but would no longer have the ability to play. No, you are not quite ready. She continued to ask again and again. Finally, the father gave in and brought the violin to her bed. He placed the bow beside it. Her head was wrapped tightly with a scarf as she picked up the violin and tucked it tightly beneath her chin. She picked up the bow. She looked at the bow and then the violin. She looked at the bow again and then the violin. She finally looked up at her father. He knew now was the time to explain it to her. But how do you explain to your young daughter that everything she knew about this joy in her life was gone? All of the memories she had once cherished were no longer hers to hold. How do you explain this when we, as adults, cannot comprehend the confusion of this loss? He never needed to explain it at all. To his awe and the awe of the medical staff, she looked once more from the bow to the violin and very slowly began to pull it across the strings. At first, she was awkward and clumsy. Soon though, her beautiful music began to fill the air. Her brain had known of the damage it was experiencing and moved the musical memory into a new area. These memories of music were still hers to hold onto and cherish forever.

Another young lady had to have a section of her hippocampus removed. The neurosurgeon explained to her this section held all general memories. Upon awakening, they did not know what memories may be lost. She went home that day. She took out a pen and a notebook. Slowly at first, and then frantically, she began to write. *This is my name. These are my parents. This is my family now. This is a map of my neighborhood. This is what I like. This is what I enjoy. This is what scares me!* She wrote down all the memories that she needed to cherish. She wrote down everything she wanted desperately to hold on to. Her surgery was fairly successful. The doctor came to her room timidly when she was waking. He asked, "Do you know your name? Do you know where you are? Can you tell us where you grew up?" And she knew! She was able to hold onto all of her memories as if she had never lost anything. Her brain, too, had known of the damage that had been done. It moved the memories before the surgeons had the opportunity to remove the small piece of her brain. Cherish your memories. Whether they are bitter or sweet, remember all the memories that make you who you are today.

I feel as if I can speak on great authority as to why you should cherish these memories. I am the mother that no longer remembers having my children. I am the patient who is missing a piece of my brain yet has a notebook of things I never want to forget. Cherish your memories. Hold onto them all. I hope that you will never have to let them go.

HEALTH

You only get one body. Treat it well.
Never take it for granted.

Psst: I Have a Secret...Go Ahead, Read It!

Shhhh. I have a secret I want to tell you. Be careful who you tell, though. You would be disappointed in the reaction of some people!

If you look at me, I appear to be petite but strong. I *am* strong... mentally. It was not that long ago that I worked with adjudicated youth. Back then, I was physically strong, too. I was trained in self-defense and could easily take a 300-pound person to the ground in a matter of seconds. Now a kindergartener can take me down with little effort. Not only have I lost my physical strength, but I have lost my balance as well. I also appear as if I can see everything in front of me. I walk with confidence and without hesitation. The truth is, I was not distracted when I walked right by you, and I was not daydreaming when I ran into the light pole. My eyesight is half gone. There is a great deal I miss now.

But these are my secrets. I have learned there is a time and place to share them. I am caught between a rock and a hard place. Upon first meeting, is it better to let you know that I have limitations, or is it more important for you to believe that I have unlimited opportunities with my apparent abilities? This is a question that goes through my mind on a nearly daily basis.

I often get asked, "What happened to your leg? Why are you limping?" Sometimes this will be said after I have known a person for a while. Other times, it will be asked upon first meeting an individual. Within the answer lies my crossroads. If I answer nonchalantly, "I always limp. I had a stroke." The first reaction is always immediate astonishment, concern, and then sympathy. I do not want sympathy. I especially do not want it when the person asking is not willing to listen to me explain that it turned out to be the greatest thing that could have happened to me. I want to explain that they should not be sad for me. Rather, I want them to rejoice with me for what I have overcome. My physical strength might fail me often now, but my inner strength is so great that it is immeasurable.

If you see someone in a wheelchair, be very careful about your initial reaction. They may be able to push the wheels faster than you can run. Very possibly they are faster and more efficient with problem-solving due to the limitations they have had to work around. If you come across someone who is deaf, be careful what you say. They can hear the unspoken language of your body better than your hearing ears will ever allow you to understand. Do not judge a disability you can quickly notice. Do not think of what you see as a weakness. The unnoticed compensating abilities that person has may shock you.

I really do not mind my limitations. Sure, it would be nice to get back some of what I have lost. However, I could never accept giving up the amazing vision that I have for my life just to regain my missing sight. I would never relinquish the inner strength that I have gained just to get back the strength in my arm and leg. Without half of my world always black as night and the left-sided weakness I live with, I would never have gained nor held on to the ability to maintain these newfound treasures I harbor within me. I wish other people could understand this upon my first encounter with them. So, is it better to let people think I am a daydreamer and laugh when I walk into light poles? Is it better to allow them to think I hurt my leg in an accident (it *was* a cerebral vascular accident, after all) or is it better to accept their pity and have them cast their generalized views of weakness on me so they allow room for my limitations? This is a dilemma I face often and will continue to weigh.

I warn you, do not mistake the limitations some people have as weakness. It will only frustrate me. But then I will change my attitude, allowing me even more determination to find great pleasure in proving you wrong! And remember: Shhhh. Don't tell my secret. I really do not want you to have to experience the unacceptable pity some people feel the need to give me.

Neuroscience Research

An amazing lady read my blog and was so inspired after reading "From Couch To Dreaming of a 5K," she pledged to complete a training for her very first half marathon! Even more to my awe and amazement, this woman offered to raise funds for a stroke-related cause of my choice! I cannot begin to express my gratitude and admiration for everything she did. I requested these funds go to a neuroscience lab that studies not only strokes but also epilepsy, brain injuries, and many more neurological conditions.

I wrote a paper to help with her efforts. This was my plea for people to support her marathon and fund-raising attempts. Neuroscience is not a familiar topic to the general public. This post was my effort to demonstrate how many lives research truly does touch. If you would like more information, please contact me.

My Guest Post

How can I adequately put together words to share a message which will provide you with an understanding that neuroscience touches many lives in many ways? It dawned on me, maybe I should simply start by telling you about my day…

I woke up early this morning. I walked outside after checking on my two beautiful daughters still snug under covers in their beds. Out in the crisp, chilly morning I stared for a moment at the beautiful, snow-capped mountains with the sun behind them just waking up to greet the day. I made breakfast for everyone. Soon, I will drive to the store to buy groceries and then come home to bake some delicious cookies. Tonight, after supper, I will kiss my husband goodbye. I will watch the girls kiss and squeeze him tight for the hug that he hopes to never release. He will place his sea bag into the car and drive to the navy pier where he will board a ship to leave first thing in the morning for a short trip. The girls and I already have plans for this week to go to a park, go for a walk, and play some extra games. I will tuck them into bed tonight. After they are drifting off to sleep, I will take one last trip around the house to check the doors and shut off all the lights. I will lay down by myself and say my prayers thanking God for the gifts I am able to enjoy each and every day as I drift off to sleep grateful for all I have.

This is a fairly normal day in some aspects. However, this life that I am blessed with is only possible because of all the research that was accomplished before I was affected with a neurological condition. Hopefully, the research I now participate in may make my previous hurdles obsolete for future generations. After all, generations ago, people with epilepsy were sent to live in insane asylums for care. Stereotypes still linger. In the late 1990s, I was invited to church by a lady who felt that my sins had allowed the devil inside of me. Her church could help purge these demons and end my seizures. As a society, we have come a long way from treating epilepsy as if it were a mental illness. Yet, we still have quite a way to go. Thankfully, I comprehended that my seizures were created from an uncontrolled medical problem within my brain. No fault needed to be placed on my parents or myself for this disorder. To this day, stereotypes remain. I was fortunate in 2003; epilepsy surgery was no longer experimental. By then, it was a nearly routine surgery, and there was medical hope.

At that point, the seizures had taken their toll. I had suffered from amnesia and lost a considerable amount of memories. I was also seizing mainly at night. If my husband had not been there to turn me over, I would have died on more than one occasion. My surgery to remove scar tissue on my brain did not go as planned. There was a complication at the end leading to a stroke. At age twenty-seven, I woke up missing a section of my brain, but having gained a new perspective on life. The struggles were many as I began a long journey to recover. I did not have a seizure for nearly eight years following my surgery. I have learned so many tricks of healing. Did you know that if you put your non-affected arm in a sling and force the side that suffered paralysis to work, it helps stimulate the brain and can help improve the recovery? Did you know that neuroplasticity (the brain's ability to reorganize itself in forming new neural pathways around the injured areas) is very possible and even more common than ever thought?

So why is it important to research the brain? I woke up this morning. I got the paper. I can wave to my husband and let him sail away. He can continue his Navy career, and I can continue being a full-time mom. Why neuroscience research? Because of research discoveries before I needed a lot of my care, I was never placed in an institution. I am not in need of twenty-four-hour care now. Rather, I am a mom who can no longer run but has the ability to hold the hands of my children and enjoy walking them to school every day. I am a navy wife whose husband can continue to serve our country because we are no longer concerned about the seizures that come at night. I am a mom, wife, friend, daughter, and someone who has the ability and hope to provide more research information and funding. Future researchers will take what I can give and offer even more hope for neurology patients still to come. These future patients will be spared some of the difficult roads others, such as myself, took. I thank you for helping me pay it forward!

The Doctors, the Girl, the Vampires

I finally gave in and attempted to catch up to our pop culture. I picked up the *Twilight* series by Stephenie Meyer. I do not usually enjoy fantasy books. I like books related to a life I could experience no matter how unlikely. Hoping I can spend an eternal life with a vampire husband goes well beyond my suspension of disbelief. That being said…I truly became engrossed in these books and was able to understand the draw at once. It took me only a few days to read each book, but the storylines lingered in my mind.

Last week I went to the doctor. I needed blood tests and was sent to a lab. I used to be terrified of needles. I do not know when it was that I became immune to the sight of them and the slight stab as it pushes through my skin. But somehow, some way, I became completely accepting of needles and the jobs they did. Maybe it was my weekly allergy shots growing up. It could also have been the regular lab work as seizure medication was adjusted again and again.

On this particular day I was sent to the lab, there was a young girl sitting across from me. I could tell she was a pro at having blood drawn. Even the phlebotomist was impressed with how still she sat. The girl knew the exact process that would occur as they prepared the needle, then filled the vial. This girl was an expert in an area so many adults fear. It made me wonder why. How many times had she sat in chairs like these? How many children become tougher than adults for many reasons we wish they could have never experienced? Was this particular girl like me and sent there regularly to check the levels of medication in her bloodstream? Did she have a condition I have never heard of (and prayed would never become an everyday household word in my home)? I hoped not, but her stillness and calmness made me feel a touch of sympathy and a lot of awe for her apparent bravery. I could only hope they would give her a fun, entertaining Band-Aid of Hello Kitty or some super hero. She was a super hero in my eyes.

The new doctor that had sent me to the lab on this particular day apparently is very thorough in her work. She left no test unchecked. My phlebotomist leaned over my paperwork and put label after label on collection vials. The other phlebotomist went through three patients while mine was still marking, labeling, marking and labeling yet again. As I sat there, my mind wandered to the book I was currently on, *Eclipse.* The suspension of disbelief was suddenly becoming easier and easier. I saw the vials and wondered if I should really lose that much blood in one sitting. I thought of the vampires and their role in these books. I looked at my friendly phlebotomist and attempted to listen to her easy chatter.

My phlebotomist that day probably felt ill-at-ease as I told her about the story of vampires and asked how much blood I could lose in one sitting. I laughed lightly as I told her I had been reading this series as I waited for her to call my name. Yet, she did not need to fear my response to those nine vials sitting between us. I was so experienced in this field I could point out the healthiest vein for her to use. If not for the stroke leaving my left hand not quite as strong and steady, I could probably do this draw myself. I did not gasp as I intently watched the needle pierce my skin. I did not even appear to be counting along as I mentally calculated the vials remaining. I remembered the awing peace and strength the little girl had displayed. If at her age the discomfort could be masked, why couldn't mine? Besides, I had a Hello Kitty Band-Aid sitting there just as I had requested. I understood the joy a simple Band-Aid could offer by placing humor into an otherwise stressful day. The doctor still would be able to run more tests. The *Twilight* series would still run through my mind. I gained peacefulness from children surrounding me. And most importantly, I knew super heroes and unbelievable strength rarely remained within the pages of a book.

Keeping It Real

Bruised but not broken

Ten years after my stroke and I still fall down. I average about one major fall every six months or so. These stumbles are common for me. I either do not see something or my left leg suddenly does not work to help keep me moving forward.

Walking occasionally still causes problems but so does not recognizing faces. I walk into a crowded room where I know I should recognize some familiar faces. Because of prosopagnosia, I sometimes do get lonely. Even in a room of friends I can feel as if I am all alone surrounded by strangers I don't recognize.

Life is not always pretty. I won't try to paint an unrealistic picture of only hope and perfection. There are still times I have to face the hard reality of stroke recovery and the repercussions that come with a brain injury. I've come to accept in this survivor's journey there are bound to be intermittent setbacks.

But, always know this: I fall. I make a choice to get back up. I get discouraged sometimes during a long day. I am realistic in my remaining shortcomings. Yet, each night when my head hits the pillow, I know I have completely succeeded in one more day of living a life well lived. After family prayers were said the night of my latest injury, I continued on my own, "Thank you. Thank you for such a wonderful life."

I fall down. I will always get back up.

New Diet Movement

I have experienced paralysis. I have been in a wheelchair. I know what it is like for the body to not move upon command – to beg for the body to move when most would welcome the opportunity to sit still.

What is the secret to the New Diet? Movement! I have found the key to my own health, both physical and mental, is movement. After I regained most of what I had lost, I acknowledged it and celebrated it so much, I had to share it with you.

Watch an infant. They rarely lie still. Their feet fly around as they kick their legs. Their core muscles work tirelessly as they move their arms and legs up and down, in and out. Young toddlers are much too fidgety to sit for long periods of time. Their bodies are anxious to move. Yet, what happens as we get older? The rush of the day creates an excuse to sit around motionless in the evening on our couches. Movement evolves into becoming a necessary, conscious decision we must talk ourselves into somewhere along the way.

For some reason, we feel we can only get started in the path to fitness by going out and buying this or that product we recently saw advertised. Yet, what does anyone really need to buy? No As Seen on TV product will guarantee instant physical results without any effort on the user's part, nor will it offer us a maintained spirit lift and weight loss just sitting in your living room. Thankfully, exercise opportunities are already all around us. Have you passed a playground? Look at all of the ways you can find movement in just this small area. Have you driven down to get the mail lately? Why not walk there and, if possible, walk to the park, too?

I have heard so many excuses of why physical activity is too hard to start and/or maintain. "I have to work too late." "I haven't jogged for years. I could never start now." "There is no way I could get my body to do that stuff at this point."

I am of the belief it is the first step that really counts. Opportunities for movement are all around us if we open our eyes to find them. Even when half my body did not work due to my stroke, I would push myself to maintain the health and strength remaining within the unaffected side.

Exercise can both strengthen the mind and the spirit. It is not always easy and enjoyable. Honestly, some days I exercise only because of the positive long-term effects I know it can offer for the future. I am lucky I have never had to deal with significant weight issues. Yet, maybe my acknowledgment of exercise healing a whole body is to thank for that. Many days last month I might have preferred not do my daily push-ups. Yet, persistence allowed me to do one hundred nearly every day. I completed 2,400 last month.

In 2003, I was told I may never walk independently again. I was told I may need assistive devices like a cane and AFO (ankle-foot orthotic) for the rest of my life. I may not enjoy every last second before my timer rings on the elliptical. I may not like the push-ups when I reach 97, 98, and 99, but I do treasure the fact I once again have the ability to walk. I like the gift of now taking notice of all the exercise opportunities the world offers which I had never before seen. I also really like being able to laugh and play while attempting to fly higher than my daughters on a swing set, while also strengthening my arms, abs, and legs. I celebrate the fact I can move.

Botox: Beauty in Stroke Recovery

I spent years being appalled by the idea someone would have themselves injected with toxins. Ironically, I made a choice to do just that. In light of continuing research with positive results in stroke patients and suggestions from doctors, it was my turn to be injected. I had two shots of Botox put into my lower left leg. One shot went into the *posterior tibialis* muscle. The other entered my *flexor digitorum longus.*

I received these shots from a neurologist in California. That morning was filled with negative anticipation. I had a lot of fear. I feared more damage would be done to the stroke-affected leg. I feared the muscle would become too weak, and I would not be able to walk out of the office independently. I feared my hyperreflexia – overactive and over responsive reflexes – would cause me to kick my leg up and dislodge the needle from the doctor's hand. I had fear the shot would not work as quickly as it had on previous stroke survivors. I feared I would not notice any difference whatsoever. Thankfully, within twenty-four hours after the shot it became obvious I had nothing to fear.

In my medical challenges, I have gained an immense amount of knowledge. Like so many other individuals, life experiences have taught me more and given me a deeper understanding than any school course I have ever taken. For example, if I had ever heard someone say "we need to watch your tone," I would have thought they were implying I was speaking rudely. I now know they are referring to my spasticity. I understand this is when my leg muscle – for me the *posterior tibialis* – is constantly contracting. This is why my leg is often cramped. I have trouble walking in the morning when I get out of bed. This is why I have nearly fallen over every morning for seven and a half years as I take my first few steps. I never before understood the *flexor digitorum longus* was a specific muscle near the back of my leg, nor did I know the overworking of this muscle was to blame for my toes constantly curling. This caused difficulty walking in anything other than bare feet or tennis shoes.

My most recent lesson in stroke recovery was that Botox can allow these uncomfortable, sometimes painful, irritations to disappear – at least temporarily! I had hope for relief, but I never allowed myself to dream of how quick and how complete this relief would be. The following morning after the shot I took one step. I took a second step. I waited and grabbed on to my dresser. I took a timid third step. Nothing! I let go and moved my leg around. I could not believe it. I walked down the hall and up again. Down once more and again back to my room. No pain or stiffness at all. For seven and a half years, I had been unable to get out of bed and not experience a need to brace myself. Later that day I put on a pair of dress shoes and did not feel discomfort when I began to walk. I had feared a lot when I went in for that shot twenty-four hours before. Maybe one thing I feared most was the unspoken fear to hope for amazing results. It was these amazing results I woke with the next morning.

I never quite understood why someone would want to alter their appearance through an injection that had the potential to kill in a large dosage. I have the mindset that wrinkles are earned and a story is told by those lines upon our face. An old proverb states, "Age may wrinkle the face, but lack of enthusiasm wrinkles the soul." In truth, I may never understand this elective procedure. I did find, though, that something changed rapidly with my own choice for Botox. The pain was gone with the new morning's light. The simple tasks I could barely allow myself to hope for after eight years were now mine without effort. I am very grateful for the beauty which pain-free mornings have offered. Botox has greatly improved my stroke recovery. To me, that is true beauty.

Exposed: Highly Contagious

*O*n June 25, 2003, I arrived early to check into a hospital for a scheduled surgery. I spent the next thirty days in a hospital and then a rehabilitation facility. The following eighteen months were filled with intensive rehabilitation therapy at different clinics. The most kindly remembered was a physical therapy center in Monticello, IA. Between the combination of these establishments and the events that preceded my lengthy visits, my life has been forever changed. At these medical facilities, I was exposed to three things that were highly contagious and will stay with me for the rest of my life: Hope, Love, and Laughter.

Hope: I was at a low point in my life. I lost many basic skills and was starting again near the same level where my children were. At the time, my daughters were only one and two-year-olds. I had a lot to relearn. Together we began practicing identical tasks. The one-year-old grasped the concept of walking sooner than I did. My older daughter became a pro at steering her mommy in a wheel chair. I had many people who never gave up on me. I had people that saw the light within my spirit and encouraged me through kind words, wonderful deeds, and unending support. One volunteer sat by my bed in Iowa City when I had lost the ability to see. She explained what was within the frame hanging on the wall. I could no longer see the picture she described. In her small gesture of giving me time, she gave me something beautiful to look at even if it was only visible within my mind. Phone calls and notes came in from so many friends. With all of these prayers and happy, hopeful thoughts being sent my way, there was no way I could not step up to meet the hopes that all these people had directed towards me.

Love: My family supported me and held me up when I could not stand alone. I also had medical providers who offered more than textbook recitations, but also caring that went far beyond their job requirements. Abby, a nurse's aide, brought a carton of Ben and Jerry's, two spoons, and a Styrofoam cup into my room long after her time clock had been punched out. I had people who shared tears of concern with me, but also provided words of encouragement that filled me with the courage I needed to battle the effects of the stroke.

Laughter: I learned that even though my smile drooped to one side because of the stroke, I could still find the sound of laughter deep within my soul. It helped that so many people gave me reason to share this laughter with the nearby world. I learned early on that even though the world may not always feel comfortable laughing with me, it was a healing, enjoyable feeling allowing myself to laugh at the little things that used to seem so big.

For years, I had suffered the repercussions of epilepsy. At times, people had meanly and naively treated me like this was a contagious disease. There were some who were fearful if they came too close to me they would catch it and suffer just as I had. Some people even believed the devil was inside my body. I knew seizures were not contagious. I knew I was not possessed. I knew they could not catch it. I was amazed, however, at what I uncovered as being very contagious: the power of Hope, Love, and Laughter! Repeatedly being exposed to these three conditions during my medical drama, I now have a power and greatness that will forever alter who I am.

The names of those whom I should thank for sharing these lessons with me are too great to begin to list. I can, however, in an attempt to repay them for sharing this wisdom, pass along my newly-acquired knowledge. If you see someone who needs a boost, if you know of someone who suffers with pain either physically or mentally, share with them these highly contagious conditions I learned during my lengthy hospital and treatment exposures. Hope, Love, and Laughter changed my outlook on the world for the better. These three gifts sped my recovery and eased the struggles I had to endure. I hope, through the lessons I was lucky enough to encounter, the contagiousness will carry over to you and help your outlook be forever altered as well.

Missing Brain – Remaining Questions

*I*n 2003, I underwent a right frontotemporoparietal craniotomy and anterior temporal lobectomy, hippocampectomy, as well as functional brain mapping to help combat the seizures that were creating numerous problems with my day-to-day life. It simply came down to this: the surgeons needed to take part of my brain, or the seizures could take my life.

The surgery was a success…in my battle with epilepsy. However, near the end of the procedure I had a stroke. Even this particular event was a great success for me. I learned some amazing skills when learning everything again for a second time. The patience I developed for my children in learning new tasks was immense. If they took extra time learning to button buttons, I completely understood. I had recently learned that task myself; it was not as easy as it appeared!

So yes, I would have the surgery again if I knew the possible outcome. For seven and a half years after surgery, I lived a life free of seizures. In middle school, I had my first "spell." Despite this complication, I had a full life and accomplished a lot. Seizures were always there. My surgery was completed in 2003. Since 2007, I was free of all medications, no longer using something that regulated my seizure activity but which also caused unavoidable, dreadful side-effects. However, as thrilled as I am with my life currently, there are questions that have never been answered. In part, it is these questions that have created my intense interest in the world of neuroscience research.

I remember a lot of my surgery. Some of the memories are very vivid while others are foggy. How can that be? In October 2002, my seizures became so bad that memories were wiped away and never again retrieved. Yet, surgeons went in and removed the brain tissue from that same area, and my memory became sharper. I woke up during surgery when they were sawing into my skull. I remember the odd sensation and knowing that it was not quite right, but also not minding. I remember not only the sound of the saw but also the dust that was being produced. I remember wondering if I was bleeding, yet laughing out loud. I told the doctor I had a whole new appreciation regarding the chalky taste of the pink medicine which calms upset stomachs. They told me to relax, hold still, and then talked to each other. How do I remember that? How do I remember the horrible, painfully loud sound of the retractor clicking and the feeling of my brain bouncing back and forth and back and forth? I remember I thought of a Jell-O mold bouncing. How do I remember feeling the aura before my first seizure and the person standing beside me saying, "Hold on, Tara we are almost done. Everything is going to be all right." Yet, I knew – I had the distinct feeling that it was not going to be all right when I came out of the seizure. How do I remember all of these thoughts even though I cannot remember being pregnant with my second child or her birth?

I understand that the stroke disrupted my thalamus. I have regained most feeling on my left side. In regaining sensations, why – for over a year – did it make the wind feel as if it were burning me when it blew against my arm and rain drops feel like needles going in through my bone?

How did this lobectomy with a CVA (stroke) result in a significant loss of sight? Can the optic nerve reconnect from the damage that was done and provide complete eyesight ever again? Was prosopagnosia linked to my eyesight loss? If so, will I be able to know my own children's faces again?

I joke often and tell people I had the brain surgery because doctors thought I was way too smart. They wanted to equal me out with the rest of the population, so they took out a nice chunk of my brain. As for now, I am grateful to the doctors for their help and someday, maybe with the help of great researchers, we will have these answers I am seeking. Until then, I am so thankful for everything that I do currently have!

Update: My seizures returned April 18, 2011. There is still no regret at all for having had the surgery to help ease my seizures.

SEIZURES

*Seizures can alter your life,
but they don't need to control your life.*

My Introduction to Seizures

*W*hen I was in the eighth grade, I started having "spells." I described them as an odd sensation that overcame my body. Next, would come a feeling as if I were in a television commercial. I knew who I was. I recognized the environment that surrounded me. I even knew all of the characters in the room. But somehow, I could not grasp that I was part of these surroundings. As I said, it felt as if I were viewing a previously-watched commercial on television; a sort of déjà vu. I was very aware of it. I felt a close familiarity to the happenings around me. Yet I knew, within my mind, I was not part of it. I was on the outside, off in the distance, peering into what I saw. Each time, quickly after the sensation would pass, I would feel tired. I would pat my face and count my fingers. It calmed me to realize I was complete.

I was sent to doctors. I was prescribed medications. I was told that maybe this was all in my head. People had hoped, as doctors had suggested, that I would outgrow whatever this was. They were hopeful to not place a label on me.

The dreaded label could not be denied for long. When I was fifteen, I had an undeniable gran mal, tonic-clonic, seizure. I was in bed trying to fall asleep. I had a "spell." As I was coming out of it, I called out to my parents. I did not feel right. I knew something in me was not okay. I patted my face and counted my fingers. The numbers did not add up. There were no longer ten. I was very scared. Then, there was darkness.

I woke up in the chilly night air. It felt as if I were floating. Somewhere off in the distance, a gruff voice was mumbling, "There she is. Tara, do you know what day it is?" Oh, how I hurt. Why was everything so foggy? Where was I? Someone help me, please, help me! I am scared. What is going on? Why can I not speak? I felt an intense level of panic start to come over me. My thoughts spinning as rapidly as my hazy mind let itself process the clues. Who is this man talking to me? I have seen him before, haven't I? "You are going to be okay," this voice continued speaking. I know that I have seen him before. It was dark and I was still very confused. His face became clearer as the fog slowly lifted from my mind and my vision. Where is my mom? My dad? I am so scared. Wait. Slow down. Why do I hurt? I am so tired. I just want to sleep.

Soon, I realized I was not floating. I was being rolled on a stretcher. Those lights flashing outside were on an ambulance. I live in a small town with a small ambulance team. All of these thoughts were processing at a lethargic speed. That voice, yes, it is familiar. He must be a doctor. No, a paramedic would be in the ambulance. This is my town. Something has happened to me. That is my uncle. That has to be my uncle. He is the main paramedic in our town. Could this be my uncle? Slowly, I was fighting to keep his words in my mind and not fall asleep. I was scared at the lack of recognition of the world around me. Yet, at that stage there was still more fright and concern as to what was happening to my body and my mind.

Seven years after this event, I married my husband. I explained to him that if I had a seizure, he should never call the ambulance. It was too frightening. The sensation itself, of slipping into a tonic-clonic seizure, was frightening enough. Knowing that I was drifting away carried with it a very fearful feeling. But I always dreaded the wakening, when I would wake to a room full of strangers asking too many questions at too rapid of a pace. These questions, these faces, and the possible answers were all beyond my level of comprehension in the postictal state. Even if I knew the people, there would be the moments of muffled confusion that would leave me all alone and scared in a room of perceived strangers. That was always difficult – waking up, unsure of where I was, not comprehending what had happened, and not being able to identify anyone who was near me when I first regained consciousness.

This continued for several years until I was twenty-seven. I had two daughters. The oldest was nearly two years old. My other daughter was four months old. One October morning, I woke up and the seizures started. Against my wishes to ever be taken to a medical clinic and be faced with strangers after a seizure, my husband made the correct decisions and took me to a hospital. It was at this hospital I was diagnosed with status epilepticus. My body started having seizures that morning and never fully recovered before the electrical storm would start again. My family's decision to take me to the hospital saved my life. Seizures lasted all day. This day of status epilepticus forever changed my life. This day of status epilepticus wiped away nearly two years of memories.

Perspective of an Epileptic Growing Up

Middle School

"I don't know what's wrong. I just feel weird. It just feels like I am in a commercial I have seen before. I know what's going on around me. I know everyone around me. I have seen them all before. I just can't join into their conversations. I just feel different, and then I count my fingers and pat my face. Then I am tired."

"An EEG...with all those cords? You cannot be serious! I can't wear that to school! Everyone's going to laugh at me! Twenty-four hours? But I don't want to. Fine! But, everyone is going to laugh and make fun of me."

High School

"Yeah, they're still happening. But please, don't tell anyone. Everyone already thinks I am weird when they see me count my fingers."

"I don't understand. I felt fine, went to bed, and woke up in the doctor's office. How did I get there? What's going on with me? A seizure? No way! But aren't those where people just flop around? I wasn't doing that. Was I?"

"What do you mean I can't drive? I just got my license! Six months? NO WAY!! That is so not fair! Why is this happening?"

College Life

"What do you mean I can't sleep in a loft bed in a dorm? Seriously, I might have a seizure and fall out? Stop worrying about me! I mean, I am fine. It's no big deal. I don't even really notice it until the morning."

"I know all these last medicines aren't doing anything for me. All right, fine. But, this one makes me feel horrible. I feel so groggy. I feel sick to my stomach. I feel like I can't help but get fat. Come on, why can't we find one that works? Why do you make me take medicine that totally is not helping? They just make me feel worse."

Early Adulthood

"Okay, fine I had another seizure last night, but they aren't that bad. I just wake up totally sore. No big deal. Really."

"Oh, dear God….That was *me* in this video tape? Was that really me having a seizure? No wonder I am so sore. No wonder everyone has always been so scared. Wow, I had no idea. Gosh that looks horrible!"

"What are these red spots around my eyes? Broken capillaries? I had always thought I was so lucky having the seizures at night. Now you are telling me I could have died from my own saliva? I had no clue. My seizures are getting worse – I know. Really? Seizures can kill a person? Me? Wow. Okay, even I am a little scared now."

"There is no way I am in Iowa! I went to sleep in Virginia. Oh my gosh that older girl is so cute! Who is she? What? Seriously!! She is mine? How? What has happened? Status epilepticus? Okay, please tell me again. How did I get here? How do seizures wipe away memories?"

"No medicine works. I have a period of amnesia. Now my short term memory is about gone. I have to leave notes of whether or not I stepped outside to get the mail or I ran the dishwasher. I just...I know it's time. I need the epilepsy surgery. No medicine has worked. I'll be fine. Seizures could quite possibly take my life. The surgery could save it."

"I remember the petit mal while in surgery. I remember knowing I was going to have the tonic-clonic. I remember the seizures. I remember knowing everything was not going to be all right. I remember the surgery. A stroke?"

Recent Years

"The stroke was rough, but well worth it. No more seizures! Finally, what more could I want?"

"Eight years and no seizures. I haven't felt this good, completely free of medicines, since I was young. Oh, I feel great! I am so thankful!"

"Last thing I remember I was sitting outside on the chair. Are my kids okay? How and why did my seizures come back? What can we do?"

"I can't drive again? What am I going to do? How can I get my groceries? How can I get my kids to the doctors if they get sick? No one from church is able to take me to the appointments? Really? Most of my neighbors forget to ask me before they go to the store. I guess I will have to ask them again. I lost my license. I have lost my independence. I can't drive. Six months."

"Vimpat is amazing! I have not felt any side effects. I guess that was a benefit to being medicine-free for so long. They have had time to develop new anti-epilepsy drugs."

"No, really I am doing great. Besides that one blip in April, the seizures seem to be gone. Of course I am still scared. Nearly nine years seizure free. Now they are back. Seizures always have been my disease of waiting. I will be okay though. I always am."

Seizures Move Me

You are not alone. You may be the caretaker, a mother or father, husband or wife. Maybe you are a person who has had epilepsy for years. Possibly you are reading this seeking information because of a recent partial complex seizure the doctor said you had. Whoever you are, you are not alone. Seizures moved you in some way. Seizures move us all. Whether it is the emotional stress creating tears that slide down your face or the physical pain causing you to wake with sore muscles strained from uncontrolled contractions, seizures continue to move us.

Seizures move me. They really do. Seizures move me mentally. They move me emotionally. Physically, seizures truly move me. I started having "staring spells" when I was in eighth grade. The first tonic-clonic struck when I was in eleventh grade. At that time, I still did not fully understand what was going on. Ignorance was bliss for me. Seizures merely annoyed me. Eventually they made me angry. I was frustrated they came and stole my nighttime hours. I was scared. I did not know when the next moments of confusion would come. Because of this ongoing dread, I labeled epilepsy my "Disease of Waiting."

I remember the first time I saw myself in a seizure. I had one taped, so I could see what caused me to wake feeling like I had run thirty miles throughout the night. Watching the video, I was awed. I hurt mentally. Suddenly I had sympathy filled with pain for what my family had observed over the years. You see, tonic-clonic seizures do not physically cause immediate pain to the person seizing. I was always aware of the aura, the first of three phases in a seizure. I knew when I was going to slip into a grand mal seizure where I would shake and twist my body uncontrollably, the second phase of a seizure. I woke with tiny red spots around my eyes from ruptured capillaries because of choking that occurred as I seized. I would be confused and concerned when I woke up, the third and final stage of a seizure. Yet, I had no memory of the pain that others assumed I was feeling. This is one comfort I would like to offer the caregivers of epileptics: The person that is lying there experiencing uncontrolled movements, gurgling and making mysterious moaning noises is not in discomfort or pain. During this phase, they cannot feel what is happening. The mind has given us a gift of making individuals unaware of anything they may feel during tonic-clonic seizures.

Please, always remember seizures can do permanent harm and must be taken seriously. In the past, I was neither concerned nor worried about what seizures did to me. I was frustrated at how they interrupted my waking hours by disrupting my nights. I did not understand how dangerous they could be until I went into status epilepticus. I was lucky my family was around to insist I receive medical attention. I woke after no less than seven consecutive tonic-clonic seizures to find part of my memory erased. Whether you are new to epilepsy or are familiar with your usual seizure pattern, if the seizure seems abnormal or lasts an extended time, seek medical attention immediately.

Seizures move everyone they touch. It is a Disease of Waiting. We never know when the next one will move us. Hopefully it never will. Usually they will be back at some point, sneaking into our waking hours or stealing us from peaceful dreams. Please remember that when you do wake, as you process the pain and sadness, concern or misery, you are not alone. Many others out there feel the same way you do. Too many people are moved by seizures.

The Devil Didn't Make Me Do It

Sex, religion and politics are taboo subjects in our culture. We all arrive at our beliefs through different paths. Regardless of my personal beliefs, I try hard to respect all opinions that are shared with me. I agree with some. I disagree with others. Everyone draws conclusions from their different experiences. Respect that. I will respect you. But don't hurt me and/or others.

Recently, I was attending a church. The lesson of the week was Mark 9. Within this, there is a verse which deals with a boy falling to the ground having what could be interpreted as a seizure. The pastor at this church taught that the son was having seizures and Jesus rescued him by purging the evil spirits from his body. After church, I went up and asked this preacher to further define his view of epilepsy and religion. He said "not all seizures, but those not medically diagnosable, could be fallen angels or evil spirits taking over the body of people who have not been born again." But, he did not feel all seizures were the work of the devil.

I kept quiet after his explanation. I needed time to really think about his comments before I reacted emotionally rather than responded intelligently. The following week I went up again after the service to continue our conversation. My hope for an unemotional discussion was quickly dashed. I asked questions about the progression of medical knowledge and miracles of healing beyond purging of the devil. After all, the blind man saw again and the lame man walked. I asked about young children who had seizures. He said the evil spirits could possess them too if they were living in a home without two believers.

I explained to the pastor beliefs like this were not only discouraging but potentially harmful. On different occasions, I have been invited to churches because they felt they would heal me from these "fallen angels". It never worked. There have been children who have even died because of the extreme religious view that seizures can be healed by laying of hands or exorcism. I also explained to him that for the first ten years, I was a child with seizures not medically diagnosed, yet I was not possessed because my parents were nonbelievers. When I became an adult, we did find the medical reason and no evil spirits fled from my body. When the neurosurgeon cut open my skull and removed my piece of brain, his medical report did not claim a swoosh of air passed him because fallen angels or a possession of the devil exited my damaged brain.

I hope this message is passed on by many and those with doubts are able to understand seizures are a medical, not religious, condition.

Please Help Me

Next time you go to the store, may I ask you to pick up some extra milk? May I ask you to help me find a solution of how to walk home from the grocery store with fresh fruit and meat so they do not spoil in the 100F/37C+ degree summer weather? I wanted to go to church last spring. Maybe you could help me find a way to get there. If my daughter were to run a fever for four days, I am not sure how I would get her to the doctor. School will be out in an hour. It is chilly and pouring rain outside. Do you think these umbrellas will be enough to keep my children dry and, at least slightly, protected from the damp chill?

One hundred and eighty days - 180. It is not a random number; rather, it is a magical number in the eye of the drivers' licensing department in most states. A person can lose consciousness from a seizure and somehow in six months they will be healthy enough to drive.

Six months is a very long time. After 180 days of good health, magically they are fit enough to drive.

If your car has to go in for repairs, do you feel lost? I recently overheard one mother tell our school's office her child would not be there all week due to their family being short one car. She was nearly crying from frustration. She would not have the car back for an entire week. The bus system could not come and pick her son up. I knew another man who was very angry his car was in the garage for three days. He would be forced to take vacation time. He did not have a lot saved up. Another woman was worried about how she would adequately take care of her children when she would need to walk so far to get groceries. I know one mom who spent an entire summer asking all of those questions. I am that mom.

If you know someone who never takes their car out anymore, ask if they need a ride. There are more reasons than just epilepsy which will leave people longing for the freedom a car can provide. I know last time I lost my license, it was one of the most difficult times I had of continuing a sense of normalcy for my family. My husband was away on a long work trip. It was only my daughters and me. I was told on several occasions, "Next time I go to the store I will let you know. You can ride along." I would see these same people, having forgotten to invite me, come home a few days later with a trunk full of groceries. I would remember the Sunday bake sale our church recently had for families in need, but then find out people were too busy during the week to take me to a doctor's appointment. One lady asked again and again if I needed to go out and get anything. I finally told her yes. When I asked for help, she told me she did not have time to go out and did not like that store. But, she encouraged, I should ask again next week and she'd see if her schedule freed up. That crushed me after gathering courage to admit I needed help.

When you lose your right to drive, you lose freedoms you may never have thought about before. You give up a level of independence you always took for granted. I even gave up simple things such as a speaking group I attended weekly. It was a pleasant outing to go and see these familiar people. It was fun to practice and utilize my passion for public speaking. Only one person offered me transportation. This man used the weekly outing as his social hour, too. I could not take this away from him. He would need to rush me home to pick up my kids from school. We lost my kids' opportunity to play community sports because games were not always close to our home, but sometimes miles away. I lost so much during those months. I gained little besides strong legs, a trimmer body, and much more compassion for those who are not able to drive.

So this, *this*, is what I am asking you to help me with. If you know someone who cannot drive, don't wait and make them ask you for help. The greatest gifts a neighbor gave to me were the calls when she said, "I am going to Target. Do you want to ride along with me?" I always tell people not to ask if they don't want company because I will never decline an outing. We (no individuals are immune to this) get busy in our own lives. Remember those people around you who are unable to be busy. People need your help. Whether it is calls letting them know you can get them a container of milk or giving them a ride to a meeting, it will mean more than you can ever imagine. Think back to the time when you had to take your car in for repairs. Think about what you would miss if you could not get a rental to use for a week. Imagine it was you who was unable to find transportation for months at a time. I would be happy to offer you help. Right now though, I am asking you to offer this same help to someone else in need of your kindness.

Lessons from the Willow Tree

*E*ight years…eight amazing years completely free of seizures! Four years…four years of my mind not slowed and my body not burdened by medication. Prior to these years, for a period of fifteen years, my life consisted of making sure I was properly medicated and being concerned when the next seizure would attack my brain. Please do not misunderstand me. Epilepsy never hampered me from living a full life. Epilepsy did, however, leave me always wondering when the next seizure would come and what adverse side effects it would create causing confusion within my body. So trust me, for the past eight years I have held onto the independence, happiness, and freedom that came with living a life free of medical conditions! Since my epilepsy surgery in 2003, not one day has been taken for granted. I have remembered how lucky I am to be living a healthy life.

Then, suddenly, I battled an unexpected – but always feared – storm. While lying in a hospital bed, I held tight to lessons that I have learned regarding the strength of a willow tree. Like the tree, I found a way to bend. I held on tight. Seizures again battered my brain and my body. Unexpectedly, I went from enjoying a beautiful spring day outside with my children to feeling a tingling sensation in my left fingers and toes. My next conscious memory was being rolled on a stretcher from the ambulance into the emergency room. I remain grateful for the strong roots I have cultivated in family and friends. For six days, I rested in a hospital bed connected to a video EEG hoping to catch some record of the electrical storm that has again taken hold of my mind. I was able to bend with this storm and still arrive on the other side with barely a bruise.

So, what are these lessons I recalled from a willow tree? A willow tree appears to hardly have a trunk. It is very small and narrow compared to its long, weepy branches. If you look at its unimposing trunk, it appears to be weak, fragile. Yet, it is not a fragile plant. It is one of the toughest. As the wind blows, as storms rage on in the world, the willow tree will bend and will remain strong. Rarely can the fierce storm cause it to break. You see, there is a secret the willow tree has learned over the centuries. The secret lies in its roots. As bendable as the willow tree may appear to be, deep beneath the earth the roots of the tree are strong, solid, and secure. The tree can bend, but it will not break because of the invisible strength holding onto what we mistake as a frail trunk. Other trees that grow strong and solid contain a massive trunk. They look mighty, but in storms they will snap. The roots will pull from the ground.

Even the sad-looking branches of a willow tree contain hope and purpose. The long, lazy branches allow room for the centered trunk to bend and space for the tree to stretch and move. We can all learn from this tree. The lessons of a simple trunk and strong roots to keep us grounded can show us all direction during the storm. My seizures have returned. My body will again need medication. I have a strong center though. The roots of my family and friends will hold me tight. My optimism will ensure I have space to keep hope and purpose. My optimism will allow me to overcome tremendous obstacles. The returning seizures will not hamper my life. Like the willow tree, I will continue to weather the storm.

Seize the Opportunity: Epilepsy Awareness Month

*N*ovember is National Epilepsy Awareness month. This is the month when everyone touched by epilepsy hopes to extend their knowledge regarding this disorder to other people everywhere. It is a time to explain what it is, how to help people who suffer from seizure disorders, and to share the idea that there is always hope for a routine, normal life. It is now my turn to participate in this goal and help share my knowledge with you.

What is epilepsy? Epilepsy is a brain disorder where an individual has any type of spontaneous seizures. Seizures are episodes of disturbed brain function which alter a person's attention or behavior. During seizures, the electrical signals within one's brain become overexcited.

Even if you were unaware, there is a very good chance that you have known someone who has epilepsy. People with seizure disorders do not wear special shirts or hold signs that say "I Seize." With the help of special diets, medication, or even surgery in the most extreme cases, seizures can be controlled. If you do see someone having a seizure, there are a few important things you can do to help that person:

1) Gently direct the person towards a safe area. Remove any sharp objects that may present danger as you guide the individual to a comfortable sitting or lying position. 2) Never, never ever put something in the mouth of a person having a seizure or attempt to restrain any part of their body. Give them space. Give them time. Offer them words of assurance when it is over. Seizures are not contagious. You will not "catch" a seizure from someone, nor will you be hurt in talking to them about it afterwards.

Here is an attempt to outline a very small portion of things an epileptic must consider. It is important to note that when seizures are properly controlled, people with epilepsy can continue living a normal life.

Regardless of the level of control over the seizures, some precautions should always be taken. Never bathe when alone in the house. A shower is the safest choice. An individual may be at-risk for drowning in small amounts of water when consciousness is lost. For this reason, swimming alone is never a good idea.

When seizures are uncontrolled, life gets much more complicated. For example, in many states, your driver's license is lost for exactly six months after having a tonic-clonic seizure. I never was able to figure out what magic happened at one hundred and eighty days! Imagine just being old enough to drive, having your first grand mal seizure and having that privilege taken away from you. Think of giving up your car tomorrow. How do you get to work? How do you make it to your doctors' appointments? Who will drive your kids to soccer practice? A severe seizure can wear down a body and may pull muscles. How do you call into a new job and explain you will not be in because your body has been temporarily damaged from an event that you cannot recall? It is hard enough to be a father, a mother, a friend, or a coworker and know that people need to be able to depend on you. It is harder when you know seizures are unpredictable and can attack when you least expect it. The seizures take away the control of knowing you will be alert and ready to provide for the needs of those depending on you.

It is heartbreaking to be the parent or caretaker and watch your loved one being pulled away into the darkness of the electric storm within their mind. How do you connect with them at that point and decrease the hurt you feel for the child who momentarily has no control over their body? I can understand it is not enough to know they cannot feel what is happening. At times, it remains nearly too painful to watch their inner storm occurring.

How can you help someone with epilepsy? Realize that seizures are common – much more so than you may have realized. A seizure will not hurt a bystander. Epilepsy is not a communicable disease. It cannot spread. As with all aspects of life, knowledge is power. Share this knowledge with everyone you know. Break the myths and offer hope through support.

Now it is your turn. In honor of Epilepsy Awareness Month, help educate others about seizures. Do your part to help spread the word. The Epilepsy Foundation is one of the many great organizations that you can visit online to find more information about epilepsy.

When Seizures Seize the Night

*N*ight falls. In the stillness, you lie in wait. Will it come tonight? Will it be bad? Will it leave me in pieces, or will it leave us in peace? Epilepsy was the thief of the night for many years of my life. I never knew when it would come. My seizures mainly struck when I was drifting off to sleep. It would fill my evenings with negative anticipation. It was always my Disease of Waiting.

It is a disease of waiting for that next unpredictable lightning strike, but it is also a medical condition that may be more painful for the observer than it is for the victim. Now, do not misunderstand me, I know that seizures can range from a mild case of moments lost to a life-threatening occurrence. I have suffered all levels. But I have also gained the knowledge of what a bystander will see as my mind slips into unconsciousness. I understand it is a blessing when our mind shuts off. Our body can thrash. We will wake confused with pulled muscles, a pounding headache, and exhausted limbs. But understand that through the suffering (I bit hard into my tongue), through the thrashing (I bruise, I may bleed), during the seizure event itself, I do not feel the immediate pain. My body has been gifted with the ability to feel nothing at all.

I have watched my seizures. After years of not understanding why I would wake so sore and confused, I finally saw a videotaped seizure event of myself. I know what you see. I have seen a severe tonic-clonic seizure from the eyes of an observer. I do understand the pain, hurt, and suffering that the seizure can cause you. I understand the wild fear that fills your eyes.

I cannot take this rightful fear away. I cannot offer you absolute calmness. It is my wish, though, that I give you this knowledge. When seizures held tight onto my body, I did not feel the pain and misery that you observed. You were the only one in the room with the ability to feel instant pain. I am sorry, caretakers, for what you have to see. I hope that by gaining this first-hand knowledge, some of that fear – even if it is just a small amount – may be able to be released. Hold onto this realization, embrace it. Some nights will remain quiet with no electrical storm in the brain. Other nights, realize that this too shall pass. It always does.

Seizures, Status Epilepticus, and Amnesia

Think of it: what would you do if you woke up and a year or more of your memories were missing? Would it be a gift or a curse? Most of us have considered at one time or another what it would be like if we could choose to erase some of our memories. We contemplate whether it would be for the better or worse if some period of our life would be wiped away as if an eraser made it disappear.

As I went to sleep one October night before my brain surgery, I remember having the first seizure. During the recovery stage, my fingers did not seem to be all there. I knew I was not going to recover from this episode. I knew to prepare my body and alert my husband that something was very wrong. A tonic-clonic was quickly approaching. Then there was a long time of nothingness.

I woke up in a hospital room. After the fog began to lift, I remember requesting the medical staff show me their ID badges. I wanted to be sure of where I was. That is when the confusion began to settle in. In my mind, I fell asleep in our rented townhouse in Virginia. My husband was stationed in Norfolk. We had an infant daughter. She was tiny with curls in her hair. When I awoke, I was in Iowa. We owned a house. We had purchased a new vehicle. My husband was no longer on a ship but now a Navy recruiter. Most shockingly though, the baby they brought into my room was no longer my only child. They also brought in a toddler with curly hair. The young baby had been born four months earlier. She was ours. My oldest was walking now. My seizure that night had not ended for hours. I had gone into status epilepticus. During those missing hours, my seizures completely wiped away over a year's worth of memories.

Upon recognizing this, surprisingly enough, I did not set into a frightful panic. It was more amazement and awe that filled me. I was even later slightly humored of my fine taste in our new house, of our nice new van, and of our ability to create such beautiful children without my knowledge.

It took a few weeks of tests and changes to my medication before I was finally discharged. My memory stayed fragile, leaving empty periods of time I cannot recall. To this day, there are many memories I never was able to recover. Other memories have come back to me. Yet, sometimes I wonder how genuine those memories are. I have kept journals off and on for quite some time. Between rereading those and revisiting pictures frequently, I am curious how many memories are really mine and how many were recreated through hope and repetitive learning.

I had to meet our neighbors all over again. I am sure it was as uncomfortable for them as it was for me. I was previously a familiar, chatty person in their eyes. Now, they were strangers I had never seen before. There have been a couple of times a conversation has come up with my family about something negative during that missing time. I've asked not to relearn those memories. Yes, our struggles do make us who we are at the present time. But really, if we all could just completely forget some things from our past, would that be so bad? Some memories are still missing, and I will be grateful if you continue to keep it this way.

PROSOPAGNOSIA

*Every time I see your face, you appear as a
stranger to me. It works in your favor.
I will give you a million chances
to make your first impression.*

Riddle: We have seven of these in our house. You certainly have some in your home. Every time you gaze at these, you will probably think they appear the same wherever you may be. When I look at them, I will always see something different. What am I?

Answer: Mirrors.

Cues, Clues, and Other News

*N*ot so BREAKING NEWS: I have prosopagnosia. I live with face blindness. It was acquired from a stroke. For twenty-seven years, I knew my friends, my family members, and my own reflection upon first glance. I no longer have the ability to recognize any of these people.

I was walking my daughters to school today. Nearly there, I let them get a block ahead of me. When I turned the corner, they were farther ahead than I had expected. And now, there were four blond girls instead of two. As always in situations like this, there was a note of concern. The usual, familiar situation had changed. The automatic response of relief knowing I was looking at my daughters was replaced by confusion, hoping two of the four were my children. Their bags were swinging in front of them. They all had on blue jeans. The profile of their faces was the only clue left for me. The characteristics I am able to recognize were suddenly of no use. Adding to the stress, there was a lady walking between me and the girls.

I looked to the ground and noticed wet footprints on the cement coming from a house half way up the street. Two small, separate sets of prints cut close to the grass. A larger print made a wide turn from the driveway to the sidewalk. This house was where my girls' friends lived. Their two daughters attended school with my children. They rarely walked. Usually their mother drove them. This mother was close to my height, but built with a larger frame than me. These clues came together and I was confident my daughters were within that group of girls. Then the sound of laughter fluttered through the air. I knew two of those giggles belonged to my children. It was a beautiful sound offering joy and relief from my concern.

I thought I saw their mom coming up behind me, I called out her name. Generally, this is an event that makes me feel uncomfortable. It is another time filled with dread for me. What if the clues did not lead me to the correct conclusion? What if this unfamiliar face is not someone I know and I have called out the wrong name to a complete stranger? I got lucky this time. I was correct about who this lady was. After chatting for a while, she again mentioned her amazement about my complete lack of facial recognition. She explained, yet again, how hard it is for her to understand how I cannot recognize people but so easily call out a name.

I explained the footprints left by the morning dew. I explained the laughter that flows from my children. I explained habits and my concern when people deviate from these patterns. I tried to help her understand anyone can do this. I never would have believed it either. Before I lost this ability, I always took recognizing faces for granted. Back then I used to focus on fleeting glimpses I could see of friends passing by. Now I focus on more detailed clues like the backpacks my children carry and footprints that offer direction of who also left their house so early on a school morning.

I do have face blindness. I do not recognize the faces of friends or family. I do not even recognize myself. Yet I now pay close attention and try hard to notice the clues a person's habits or patterns provide, cues I see within body language, and other news I can gather together that will hopefully help me call out the correct name of a familiar stranger.

Noticing Your Eyes – As Altered By Prosopagnosia

Facial expressions are as readable since acquiring prosopagnosia as they were when I could still identify faces. Other nonverbal clues require developing more attention to specific details. By looking at the eyes of people passing by, I can learn a significant amount. Some people will flat out ignore me. Others will intentionally avoid eye contact. This is most often noted when people are looking in my general direction. Once they are close enough to make out my frame, they look away and keep their eyes diverted while we pass each other. These people, I often think, are either shy or nervous or have another reason they would want to avoid any potential conversation. Most people will at least glance at a passing person. When someone does not know me, they look my way and generally nod their head, and then find another object to look at as we pass. Their walking pace neither slows down nor hesitates. It remains constant. If someone does know me, I find they usually raise their chin a few millimeters, slow their pace, and engage in eye contact for an extended time. At this point, I realize a connection has been made. We exchange a hello. If nothing more is said on their part, I begin seeking verbal clues.

With face blindness, I still see a complete face. I can see all the details the same as anyone else. The difference is I have no ability to remember whose face I am looking at. I need to gather extra information I never before would have taken time to notice. Finding clues has now become the main technique I use to recall someone's identity. It has been proven when we lose one sense, our remaining senses become stronger to help compensate for what is missing. I have come to believe this is true about memory also. I lost the ability to remember faces. I compensate by being able to notice and remember smaller details now. I take note of what previously would have been thought of as an insignificant detail. There is one little girl I see who tilts her head down and lifts her eyes up any time she speaks to an adult. There is a receptionist I often see sitting at her desk who starts speaking to people before she attempts to make eye contact.

Details: They hold the clues allowing me to compensate for not knowing your face.

~

Defining Communications –
As Altered By Prosopagnosia

*W*hen I was twenty-seven, I acquired prosopagnosia. Prosopagnosia is the inability to recognize faces of familiar people. This condition is also known as face blindness. While growing up, I was always able to identify familiar people walking towards me. Unfortunately, at twenty-seven, I lost the ability to be able to identify my family, my friends, and even my own reflection.

I lost my ability to know someone when I looked at them, but I became better at picking up cues from emotions people display on their faces. I began to depend more on recognizing clues I observed while speaking with individuals. Using these clues, I am aided in recognizing familiar strangers without needing to depend solely on recognizing their faces.

Communication is a word we all use. Everyone knows its meaning, but we often forget about the simplicity behind the definition. Communication is when a message is sent by someone or something and received by at least one other person. Upwards of 97% of what we communicate is done not through spoken words but how these words are received.

Think of this sentence: "Yeah that was interesting." Four simple words which are often said. Take the time – I dare you to even look at yourself in the mirror – and try this. First, say those words while thinking of something disgusting like eating repulsive foods on a national television show. Now say those words while having admiration for the young genius that can recite pi beyond the thousandth digit. Again, say those four words while thinking of your boss announcing that half of the employees are getting a substantial pay raise next week and you are among that half. Now say the words as if you just walked past a group of kids cussing profusely. In every scenario, your tone has changed greatly. The expression in your eyes will be altered. The four words never changed. However, the tone that was used and the response in your eyes offered a very telling clue to what was being said beyond the words. In the same way, when people communicate with you, a lot can be heard beyond specific words that are spoken. Once this is understood, you can learn to tell so much about the message a person is conveying to you.

With prosopagnosia, I may not be able to recognize a face, but the emotional characteristics held in that face are recognizable. I still can read the tears and frown as sadness. I still can be aware if there is deep rage within someone's eyes and know that they feel anger. Recognition skills are still available for emotions. Auditory skills erase any doubt I have of possibly mistaking the visual clues about emotions. The sudden gasp of air along with the mouth shaped as a tight, round circle indicates surprise. The fast chatter, raised pitch of a voice, and eyes moving quickly along with the eyebrows slightly raised will tell me that someone is anxious or excited. Even though I may not have the recognition of who the face belongs to, there is still a message being conveyed to me that is demonstrated by the face I see.

The World Needs Name Tags

*L*ast week I went to a work party with my husband. Around forty people, some familiar and some strangers, crowded into a small room and were mingling about. With conversations surrounding us, all the voices blended into one. It was difficult to pick a familiar voice from within the group. In other words, a nice night out was slipping into a frustrating experience of "have I met you before?"

With prosopagnosia, how do you find out who each person is? How do you comfortably move among forty people all saying hello to one another and nonchalantly ask each of them, "Hey, do we know each other?" You don't. That is the problem with social gatherings. Unless you want to stand before everyone and make an announcement regarding the condition also known as face blindness, you have to merely fake it until you make it. Sometimes there will be a distinct characteristic of an individual that will allow you to recognize them easily. Sometimes a person will give you enough information about their life that you will be able to identify how you know each other. Some individuals with prosopagnosia find identifying these clues too challenging and frustrating. They choose to stay at home and remain in their peaceful comfort zone. This is not my nature. I long for social companionship. I cannot let the world of strangers deter me from taking in all the joys I previously knew before acquiring prosopagnosia.

As we arrived at the party, a gentleman said hello to me. It was then I began to analyze who he was. 1) He knew my name. 2) There was no confusion or reluctance filling his eyes as he greeted me. This told me he was familiar with who I was. He knew me, so I must know him. His question of how I was, was genuine. His mannerism showed kindness and courtesy. The most telling clue was his speech. It held an accent of someone raised in the southern United States. Ah, yes, I was now sure I knew this man. Yet, before I started inquiring about his wife and children by name, I leaned into my husband's shoulder and quietly whispered the name asking if I was correct. Yes, I was. With this confirmation, we went on to have a very nice conversation.

Name tags would be so helpful in situations like this. Then again, name tags would be helpful any time I step out my door. What is it like to have prosopagnosia? It is intimidating. It can be disappointing. It is a mixture of frustration and sadness at times. Yet, many times I find the humor lying behind my initial solutions. Expecting the entire world to wear name tags for us is a bit too much. Rather, I think I should fill my closets with shirts stating, "Please let me explain prosopagnosia to you...unless I just did." I do not resent having face blindness. It is currently estimated 2.5% of the population has it. I am not alone.

I am not alone in the world with this condition, but sometimes it is astounding how alone I can be in a crowded room. If I know you, please say hello. If I ignore you, please do not assume I was being rude. Saying, "Hi Tara. How are you? I'm Susan," will help me a lot. Do not feel awkward about this frequent introduction. After all, I remember your kindness. I remember our previous conversations. I remember your joy and my response of excitement. It is just that I do not remember the appearance of your face. I continue to wish we could all wear name tags whenever we leave the house. I know it may be too much to ask for, but it would be nice to never again have to guess who the kind stranger is at a gathering. If it is you, I really hope you come over and say hello again. Whether it is the first time or the twentieth that we have met, I will be grateful to learn your name...again.

The Seizure – The Cop – The Prosopagnosia Experience

A neighbor phoned me. "Tara, my wife just called. She thought she was going to have a seizure. I called the ambulance. Can you go up there and check? I am on my way home."

This family is not new to epilepsy, but it is still concerning when seizures occur. I ran up there as quickly as I could. The ambulance had already arrived. By the time I reached the front door, paramedics had started their assessment. The stretcher was slightly inclined, facing away from me. As they turned her, I could see her eyes were closed. It appeared she was peacefully resting. Except, it was obvious the questions these paramedics were asking were not getting through to her. Saliva had run down the side of her face. I was assured she was okay other than being postictal (the last period of a seizure when the brain is recovering). As she was being rolled out, I heard these men say to her, "Tell us your name. Do you know where you are?"

I told her, "Don't worry about answering the questions. You are safe. You're going to be okay. These guys are going to get you looked over. You had a seizure, but you are going to be fine." Then I turned towards the paramedics and quickly said, "Those are scary questions to wake up to. Start by addressing her by name, and then tell her where she is now and where you are taking her. Don't expect her to know. She is not aware of anything right now. Please, don't scare her. Help by comforting her, and then ask your questions after you can see she is awake. The way you are asking is very, very intimidating and makes it harder to adjust to the frightening situation she will wake to find." These men must have thought I was speaking out of turn. They immediately asked me to go home and wait. They said they had to take her now and get her checked. At that, they slammed the ambulance door and stayed parked for another five minutes. I knew they were just doing their jobs and following the procedures they had been taught. Unfortunately, I also knew this peppering of questions is the scariest way to wake when you lose track of time and find yourself surrounded by an unfamiliar environment. I was not speaking out of turn; rather, I was speaking as a patient who woke up too often on that cold, terrifying stretcher.

Then I was left to wait. My neighbor who asked for help is a police officer. That is how he was able to dispatch the ambulance so quickly. He is lucky; his workforce takes care of one another. Soon after the ambulance doors closed, I saw emergency lights coming down the street. A second police car quickly turned our corner. Then another one arrived. Three doors opened. Three frantic men stepped out, each wearing a tan uniform with a hat. These three men gathered near the front door, anxiously looking up the street, then at the ambulance and then at each other over and over again. I could not tell if they were waiting for the husband or if he was one of the anxious officers looking around. With prosopagnosia leaving me with no ability to recognize a face, this situation became a lot more intimidating. Do I just limp up towards them and ask, "Does one of you live here?" Do I ask, "Which one of you just called me?" Do I say, "I walked up here and she looked peaceful. Have you seen her yet?" Possibly the husband familiar to me was not here yet. Maybe I should wait.

I had been fearful of needing to speak with cops since face blindness became a part of my life. I never expected it in this context though. Normally my worry is developed from thoughts of having to identify someone or recall specific details of a person after a crime. I never thought of the cop being someone I knew. I never expected the situation not to be about a crime but about a bad seizure. I had to watch someone suffering just as other people previously had to watch me. I waited for one officer to approach me and speak first. He said thank you, and through his voice I knew this was the man who called me only minutes before.

My neighbor was okay and returned home later that day sore and tired. Concern left my heart and awe filled my mind. The seizure: Once again I realized truth in these words, "A seizure is much more painful for the bystander observing it than for the one experiencing it." The cop: Luckily, he identified me. There was no need for me to notice specific details...this time. It is still an intimidating feeling and thought though. Prosopagnosia: It is not a disorder that only shows itself every now and then. Rather, it is a lingering condition that I notice every time a person walks by me.

A Frightened Stranger in the Mirror

This week a near run-in with a lady made me gasp as I stepped back in surprise. I was polite and apologized for our near collision. She reacted exactly as I had. I noted fear in her eyes. We had not expected to be so close to each other as we rounded the corner. Her hand slid to her mouth quickly like mine had. I knew she was attempting, as was I, to conceal a small, startled sound from escaping her lips that would draw attention. There we were nearly nose to nose. We jumped, we locked eyes and there was identical fear that could be noted between the two of us. Not fear stemming from anticipated harm, but fear developed from nearly running into each other in the compact store aisles.

Even though I am constantly aware of my condition – prosopagnosia – images of a stranger can still create surprise, humor, and fascination. The woman I faced this week as I went around a pillar in a shop was not a stranger at all. Rather, the lady was my reflection in a very tall, wide mirror. I did apologize to a stranger who was as startled as I was. In this store I, yet again, made an apology everyone could hear...to my own reflection.

I assume you are curious how I could not know myself and how I came to realize this was my own image. I do not keep a record of every time this has happened to me. Trust me, it happens often. My image has been a stranger many mornings in the mirror, in unfamiliar houses where I believe a stranger is near me as I pass a mirror I never knew existed, or as I try on new clothes and do not connect this face attached to the newly-outfitted body as the person I had just seen. I never maintain a memory of what I look like. When I have the expectation of a female with similar characteristics to be looking back, I have no doubt it is me. In the mall, there are many mirrors in unexpected places. These are the times I truly realize the extent of my prosopagnosia and how it has taken away a significant part of my memory of how I appear.

This week was one example of how my reflection becomes a complete stranger when an unexpected female surprised me. I saw her eyes. She registered surprise instantly. I understood the discomfort she felt considering how close we had come to running into each other. I next noticed her glasses. I wore similar glasses that day. They were a narrow, gold frame. I quickly glanced down to see how close our feet had brought us to colliding. Her shirt was a black, sleeveless blouse. Her shorts were a tan material. By this time, I had already said how sorry I was. Everything started to register. I had tried on two different tops that morning. I decided on the black sleeveless blouse. That day, I wore shorts rather than jeans because of the high temperatures. We were wearing identical outfits and had the same style of glasses. All of these thoughts, all of this processing, were completed within a few seconds. I knew this stranger. I did not know her appearance, but I knew the surprise and shock she felt instantly. We had the same haircuts verifying it was me! I turned away and quickly glanced around to see if others had watched this awkward exchange. I laughed – not a quiet laugh but more my cackle relieving my embarrassment and expressing humor I truly felt.

Every day I see myself I am a familiar stranger. I do not see the visual resemblance between the memory of what I look like and reflections from the passing mirror. I do comprehend what this reflection feels. There is confusion, uncomfortable humor, amazement, and fascination with the reality that she is me. All of my life I have had mirrors. Most days I notice my reflection as I style my hair and put in contacts. The person in my mirror is someone I should know. A reflection I knew for twenty-seven years. This reflection is now a stranger. I have no doubt several people in the busy store saw me apologize to the mirror. I have no doubt their curiosity was raised. So is mine when I, once again, come to understand this familiar stranger is me.

Not As Entertained By TV Entertainment

L aw & Order is no longer one of my favorite shows. I also used to regularly enjoy *CSI*, but I no longer watch that either. I have never watched a full episode of *Sex and the City. Desperate Housewives* offers me no entertainment value whatsoever. Which shows do I now try to tune into every week? *NCIS* and *Big Bang Theory* are great. *Psych* is another favorite.

I had previously wondered what it was about these shows that so strongly pulled my attention. Yes, I enjoy a good drama. Crime shows have always captured my interest. But what is it about these particular shows? Why do I no longer get enjoyment from CSI and Law & Order?

Prosopagnosia, or face blindness, is what created this change. Understanding that my inability to remember a face developed seven years ago easily explains my current choice of favorite TV shows. Those I direct my attention to now have similar, yet very different, casts. They all have both males and females in leading roles. The races vary among leading actors. If there are two people of the same gender and race, their age difference makes them easily identifiable. What is also important is the cast rarely includes guest stars. While it is nice to have an occasional guest, the rotating and unexpected characters usually leave me wondering who someone was and what role they were playing. More than once I have watched a show and lost interest when trying to identify whether the actor being shown was the lawyer or the criminal we saw earlier.

For these reasons, I also find many movies difficult to follow. I will take a book any day over something I have to watch. With a book, I can create my own images through the written words. Words are always easier to follow than a screen of rotating, unfamiliar faces.

Prosopagnosia awareness has recently increased due to media coverage and confessions of famous people such as Dr. Oliver Sacks in *The Mind's Eye.* I hope major television networks take notice of this disorder. I would love to join a water cooler conversation about last week's episode of *Grey's Anatomy.* However, when the characters all look the same to me, I am left with nothing to add to their conversation. I won't stand at the cooler and tell you about the trouble I had attempting to follow the story line, or about how many cast members lacked unique identifying characteristics. Maybe I will interrupt and ask if anyone caught *Big Bang Theory* last week. Or better yet, have you heard Pink's new song? Nate Ruess sings with her. Did you know he is from the band Fun.? (And yes, Fun. does have a period as part of their name.) I am still able to join in conversations with others regarding pop culture topics. It is easier for me to talk about music or books. I just attempt to change the subject until I find something both of us are familiar with and can discuss.

BrainStorming

The Joke I Never Told

A mother is picking her kids up one day early in the school year. A man walks by, smiles kindly, and says hello. The next day, the same man walks by with thin rimmed glasses, a plaid shirt, and khaki slacks and not only says hello but this time raises a hand for a high-five from the youngest girl which she returns with a big smile. A block later the mom says, "Who was that man? Do you know him?" Both daughters look up with joyful eyes, smiling. They were waiting for the punch line. And waiting. "Mom," the youngest says, "that was my teacher last year!" They both giggle and continue walking. I smile, helping them believe I was being silly again. I smile at the joke I never meant to tell.

This was not a joke, though. This was not a story to humor my little ones after a long day at school. This was a reality I face too often. People I should know, familiar individuals with whom I have spent many days conversing, are no longer familiar to me. I laugh at my presumed silliness, but I also shake my head considering how many friendly relationships I have passed over when someone assumes I am ignoring them or not responding in a friendly, familiar manner. As I quietly passed by the former teacher, he probably assumed I wanted nothing to do with him now that he was no longer part of our everyday lives. That was untrue. He seemed to be a very nice man. I was not trying to be unfriendly as I cautiously glanced at him giving a high five to my child. I was just unaware we had met.

This distance and difficulty in fostering friendships is also noticed online. Social media is a good way to reconnect and open doors to people from the past that miles have left distant. I became active in the world of Facebook. I was excited to find people from years ago. I discovered that even this connection of not being face-to-face still held challenges due to my lack of ability to recognize people. I remember putting in names of long-ago friends. There were multiple results for some of the people. Every result within this list had a photo next to it. None of these faces looked familiar. No connections were to be made in the instances where multiple results came in for a single name. Even through words, even through distance, the effects of prosopagnosia continue to follow me.

I will continue attempting to reconnect with people from my past and those I have just met. I will continue laughing at the "jokes" people around me assume I told. There are no outward signs you can see showing I am struggling with prosopagnosia. I seem silly. I appear to be absent-minded. Regretfully, sometimes I appear rude. To some I may even seem to be standoffish. I really don't mind if you laugh with me. I just hope you won't mind if I ask for your name a dozen times… or maybe two.

Beautiful Lady at My Husband's Side

It is rare that I am dressed so nicely. It is rare I receive a posed picture of myself from months past with no note attached to indicate the event where the picture had been taken. What is not rare is my inability to recognize myself.

I opened an attachment emailed to our home from my husband's work account. There in the picture was a formal group photo. I had no clue who these people were. My initial recognition was it was a military function. This was probably a dinner or other public event because of the uniforms being worn by the military members. The background was definitely not a ship. The civilian female was attractive and dressed for a night out rather than a day on the pier. I guessed her to be a civilian due to the fact she was the only person not wearing a uniform. That is where my recognition ended. Finally, I realized the man beside her was my husband – clued in because it was sent from his email address. He was smiling, maybe a proud smile. But who were the others with him? This remained a mystery.

I closed the attachment, hoping to remember to ask him next time he was home from work. It did not bother me that at his arm was a pretty lady. He attends events all over the world when he is away. He has pictures of himself riding elephants in Thailand, of re-enlistment ceremonies overseas, and some include various people I have never met. This lady was happy. It was a nice picture to see.

I spent the day recounting where my husband had told me he was going in his fine, dress uniform. I thought and thought and thought. It was not until hours later I remembered he had worn that particular uniform to a fancy dinner in Coronado. I noticed the other men were decorated with more medals and wore officers' uniforms. Maybe they were his superiors. Using a process of elimination, I recognized the other two men pictured must be his executive and commanding officers! Finally, my mystery was unraveling. The most recent dinner was when he was being congratulated for his participation in the Sailor of the Year program. Wait...I was at that dinner! I ran back to my computer and reopened that email. Why, yes, I do have that dress. I had only worn it once or twice. The hair cut looked like one I had. The glasses were my new ones I had recently purchased. Wait...that was me!

It is rare for me to be dressed so nicely. It is rare for me to smile and pose as I wait for my picture to be taken. But what is not rare is the disappointment only masked by humor that occurs when I find I once again was not able to recognize my appearance. Sometimes I wonder if I'm altering my appearance so often now so I will not be able to fault myself for the lack of recognition. I have two completely different pairs of glasses: one is a gold-rimmed pair that I wear to formal activities. This was what I was wearing in the photo. The other is a fun, red pair that turns to sun glasses. I also wear contacts on occasion. My hair can be pulled back, left with a little curl, or I straighten it other days. I do not seem to take my appearance too seriously. I know that tomorrow I may get a picture of a stranger, maybe even a beautiful lady on the arm of my husband. I am just thankful that when I do finally gain recognition of who that lady is, I am usually quite pleased at her quiet beauty that I never remember I hold on to.

ADDED NOTE: I realized right before I published this article that I used "her" in the last sentence when describing myself. That is one thing I notice often. When I describe a picture of myself or see a video

I am in, I describe the person pictured in third person using "she" or "her." Yet again confirming the distance I feel from my visual recognition of myself.

Flying with Loneliness and Face Blindness

I find it comfortable to be in the presence of strangers. I enjoy the opportunity to meet new people. I thrive on the ability to learn about different places and different cultures. I rarely find myself lonely when in the company of people I am not familiar with. Generally, it is easy for me to start a conversation with nearly anyone. Rarely do I feel lonely. The airport, though, is one place I most often feel the loneliest.

Even at the airport, I feel ease in conversing with people. I am captured by stories of where an individual may be going or what adventures await them at their destination. There are strangers all around me. It is the layover and the second plane that usually causes stress to develop. Take for instance a recent experience that I had flying from the west coast to Minneapolis. After that, I boarded a small plane to take me to my final destination in a smaller community.

During the first flight, the lady on my left was rather chatty and very kind. She said that she would be on the next flight I was taking, along with her sister. The man to my right was a nicely-dressed business man who was cautiously quiet. I enjoyed sharing conversation and quietness with these two individuals for the four hour ride. Upon departing the plane, I knew I would see them both again soon. The man was expecting to board a plane only a few gates from mine. Due to a thunderstorm, all flights were delayed. I looked forward to finishing a conversation I was having with each of them.

That anticipation to finish our friendly chat ended abruptly when I found an empty seat at the gate. I was lost in the sea of new faces. All of these people looked familiar, but no one looked like a person I had spent extended time talking to only moments before. In my haste of the flying rituals, I had not taken time to observe what the lady was wearing. There were several women sitting around in groups of two or more, so I could not effectively determine which might be sisters. The man had been wearing khaki pants and a blue button-up shirt but so were a few other men. My traveling companions were now lost; I was once again surrounded by complete strangers.

However, being surrounded by complete strangers is different when you know you are familiar with people in the room. Due to conversations minutes before, you know they expect you to remember them. With prosopagnosia, seeking out faces of people I have just spent hours talking to becomes extremely difficult. Once we have stepped apart from each other, I cannot recognize these individuals. Nor can I meet a fellow passenger and say, "When we step off the plane, say hello again because I suffer face blindness." No, this would not be understood in a general conversation. Yet, it is still intimidating sitting near someone and beginning a conversation without knowing if you have just talked to that individual for hours.

"Where are you heading to?" This question can be answered with a look of concern and dread if it is the same lady that just spent two hours telling you about the anniversary celebration she has been so eagerly anticipating for this trip. "How are you?" This is a difficult question in case this was the man who just explained to you how he suffered a mild case of food poisoning when he was at his last meeting in Tokyo and was thankful he was feeling better.

Yes, traveling is a fun activity I wish I could experience more regularly. However, with prosopagnosia the flight alone can create difficulties and loneliness. For, as I realize my enjoyment of turning strangers into friends, I realize it also can make me feel more lost and alone than ever. Maybe I will be lucky enough to meet you on the plane. Maybe you will be kind enough to share your stories with me. If we are lucky enough to sit together, please do not be offended if I ask you where you are headed twice in one trip.

Prosopagnosia Humor

*I*t is okay to laugh. That is what I want everyone to know. Because you feel like laughing at a particular situation brought on by my limitations, I will not assume that you are laughing at me. I always feel bad for people who are uncomfortable and appear to experience regret the moment a smile slips onto their face or a muffled, unexpected laugh escapes their lips. For me, it is healthy to find the humor in events. I encourage you to laugh with me. For example, prosopagnosia can be awkward at times. When you realize – yet again – that the person that startled you in the mirror was not a stranger invading your home but rather your own reflection, it provides a slight level of discomfort and regret. Still, it is okay to laugh about it. Take the following story for instance. How many people do you think saw this event at a local mall and thought I was a bit odd? How many people do you think wanted to laugh?

Even small alterations of my looks can cause disruption in the slight familiarity that I have in recognizing my own face. I quickly became aware that I should not alter my looks too drastically within a short amount of time. I truly gained an understanding of this on a day I had my hair cut, colored, and styled. As I left the salon in the mall, I realized that a lady was walking too close to me. She was close enough that I felt my body space was being invaded. Our eyes quickly met. I moved away and she did, too. But out of the corner of my eye, I realized she was still following me. Soon we were walking in-step too close together again. At some point, she was so close that I felt her shoulder brush against me. I swatted my hand at her. It was then that my hand hit the mirror. That was not some lady walking too close to me. Rather it was my own reflection in the mirror! I stopped and stared. She – I – looked so different. The body shape was the same, but it was as if I had never before seen myself from the shoulders up. It is a moment that is hard to capture with words. There was absolutely no self-recognition! It was this precise moment that I learned to never make drastic changes. For days, I spent time looking in the mirror trying to find at least one familiar feature in the face that was looking back at me.

Because of events like these, I rely heavily on other people's comments and opinions. Never before did I care what people thought about my hair or my clothes. Now I hang on every word that may be said about how a new shirt brings out my eyes, or how the length of my hair makes my facial features look better or worse. It is not so much that I crave to please these people; rather, I yearn for the chance to see what they recognize as the consistent appearance I can no longer easily perceive.

No, I do not always recognize the person in the mirror looking back at me. I no longer make drastic, quick changes to my appearance. And now, I always make sure that the person walking too close to me is not preparing to swat at me when I swat at them. After all, it would be a comical error to push away from myself yet again in a crowded area! I know that I chuckled. It is okay if you do too!

BRILLIANT QUESTIONS

It is a vast world. Never stop learning and growing. Never stop asking questions.

Me a Motivational Speaker? I Hope Not

$\mathcal{L}$ ate last week, I was asked, "Are you a motivational speaker?" I didn't even hesitate when I answered, "I hope not."

Do not misunderstand me – I have listened to some amazing motivational speakers. I have felt chills as they energized me to run from the room and hurry to go accomplish my goals. I have wanted to set the world on fire as they predicted I could. On my business cards, it states "motivational speaker and author." Yet, just as life changes around us, I evolve, too. When I speak, I no longer strive to make you want to run from the room to sell the next 10,000 pieces of your product, stop your bad habits, or set fire to your world.

Rather, I want to offer you seeds. As I reach a greater audience, I have realized I want to provide more than a quick touch of motivation and magic. When I am invited to speak to your large group, your classroom, or a small dinner setting, I have three goals I set out to achieve. I want to 1) Make you laugh at the silliness and entertainment life can offer; 2) Make you cry with the acute realization life can and will deliver powerful setbacks that will take a lot of work and determination to overcome; 3) Make you think about the lessons I have offered for years to come. I want to plant a seed for you to carry forever.

Everyone is at a different stage in life. This is what offers the harmony and balance as we meet new people. This is what gives us the love and compatibility as we grow our closest friendships. You might not be there yet, but someday you will touch on a lot of experiences I recount. Whether you have never been there or you are no longer facing similar adversity, I want to provide you with a seed of knowledge I have gained from my own life trials. I want to plant this seed in you leaving a pathway directing tragedy to grow into triumph when we use optimism to conquer obstacles. I want to offer you not motivation for the moment but lessons that somewhere, someday, will be remembered throughout your lifetime.

Maybe, rather than the classification of motivational speaker, I should begin a new category of a "seed-planting speaker." I have learned my true desire is not so much that I want to offer you motivation; rather, I hope to leave you thinking while I plant seeds that can help offer you strength and hope in the weeks and years ahead.

Why I Enjoy Interviews

People ask why I subject myself to interviews for the world to read and watch.

People want to know how I prepare myself for unexpected questions that often deserve revealing answers.

I am grateful to accept interviews and sit in front of a microphone because I was once the person searching for these answers. No matter how many books I read or papers I flipped through, I could not find anyone who shared their similar experiences. When I was trying to learn more about seizures, the personal interaction I had with other epilepsy patients was nearly nonexistent. I had never met a stroke victim let alone a young stroke survivor. I had no instruction booklet preparing me on how to walk confidently in a world that was suddenly only filled with strangers. The answers I sought are the ones I now hope to pass on to others.

I know what it is like to be the person desperately seeking answers. I remember, and still experience, the challenge of suddenly needing to ask questions I never before had imagined but not being able to find a person with first-hand experience on the subject.

Why do I subject myself to this? Why do I allow myself to become so vulnerable all around the world? I do it so you know you are not alone.

Also, when I am asked questions, it also helps me learn more about my own conditions. Often life happens so fast we do not take time to think of how and why we respond to challenges the way we do. Your questions make me slow down and really think about how I have journeyed from a victim to someone who not only survives but thrives.

You knocked on the door. I answered.
You have talked. I have listened.
When you ask your questions, I will respond.

Question & Answer

I have an aunt who suffered from different side effects from brain surgery, but lived the rest of her life unhappily. What has been the key to keeping a positive attitude in your life? –Bryan P.

Maybe there is something in some of us that make us more resilient than others. Maybe there is something some are born with, allowing them to be able to embrace challenges. People often tease me, saying my youngest will be my most trying child because of her strong personality. I laugh and usually reply that I have a feeling she will be my easiest. She doesn't hide things. She rarely backs away. She is more like me when I was young. Her attitude is "I shouldn't? Why? Oh, it doesn't seem that bad. Give me my consequences. Let's get it over with. I am going to do it anyway." We forge forward, and then we move on with no looking back and rarely with remorse.

It has always been my intention to live life to the fullest. I was once told you will regret more the things you don't do than those you do. As years pass, I look back with fondness and see a lot of truth in this lesson. I have lived a full, rich, and rewarding life. Yes, I have stumbled along the way and have had to go around a few road blocks. I am lucky I've always been ready to take on life. I am thankful I've always had a spirit that is willing and able to embrace challenges.

I saw a lot of people come and go while I was in the rehabilitation wing of the hospital. It always made me sad when some people yelled at the physical and occupational therapists saying they did not want to get out of bed. Getting out of bed was hard for all of us because of the challenges that had brought us in there. It was painful for some and stressful for all. I knew getting up was the only path that would lead to my recovery. After all, I was just relearning how to walk, learning how to use my hands and arms, and learning how to pronounce words. The thoughts I attempted to maintain regarding therapy: Really, life? That's all you got? Bring it on. I will smile and readily accept this challenge.

Like the younger me and now my daughter, I wasn't going to hide from this, and I definitely was not going to back away. It was another opportunity to forge forward and embrace yet another challenge.

What message would you have for us as we leave college and enter the "real world"? – John F.

Sometimes, during class visits, I tell about the time I rode the trolley by a college in San Diego. I was on this trolley with my young children when a bunch of college students all crammed in on their way to a game. They were screaming, laughing, not being all that appropriate, having a blast, and were oblivious I was there with young kids. I was irritated.

Then, I don't know how or why it hit me so strongly, I had the realization these students were who I had been not so long ago. Somehow I went from a recent college graduate – someone in the "real world" – to a wife and mom of two little girls, to losing my memories and my ability to do nearly everything alone – all within such a short timeframe.

How did this happen? How did I grow so quickly from being in their shoes into this person I had become? Life happens and we don't even see it pass by us. I had an awful lot of stuff thrown at me really, really quickly. The "real world" was rough. Yet, there I was surrounded by such beauty. The innocence of these students surrounded me as they went on their way to tailgate. Here, also, were my beautiful children I had created who were excited and awed to see these rowdy, older kids. This is life. This is the "real world."

When you leave college, take some lessons with you. Leave some things behind. Remember to laugh till you have tears rolling down your face and your stomach hurts. Forget the luxury of having the choice to sleep in and not go to work or class. I promise life will pass you by if you don't consciously make the choice to go and experience it first-hand. Cheer for those you celebrate but do not boo those you oppose. You don't know if – or more likely when – you will be in their situation someday. You may need these opponents to help you get on your feet again. The "real world" will often give you chances to start over. Never make the mistake of leaving anyone behind.

And one more important lesson: Breathe. Enjoy this moment. Sit back and smile. You're here. You have made it a long way already. Be proud of who you are, who you have become. Never forget to answer the door when opportunity knocks. There is going to be fear. There will be moments of confusion as you wonder where all the time has gone, but those are the moments you can especially realize how lucky you have truly been.

What was your outlet or stress reliever when you were first trying to figure out how to live this new life? Was there ever a moment when you were at peace with what had happened? – Erin H.

I was so busy learning how to best utilize what still remained after my stroke, I had neither the time nor the need to find a stress reliever. I was filled with awe after understanding the ramifications of having a stroke. Before this, I had never truly understood what a paralyzed person felt. Now, better than a textbook description or a movie portrayal, I am able to fully understand what it means and what it feels like. I had never understood the degree of how strongly another sense takes over when you lose one of your five.

My ability to hear returned first. It is amazing how fine-tuned your hearing can become when you can no longer see. I gathered little bits of knowledge that would help me later. I could hear how feet hit the ground differently with every step an individual takes. When you have time to really listen, you become acutely aware of whose feet are walking close to your doorway just by the sound their feet create. I knew the nurse who walked so softly her feet barely made a sound and the other nurse who took too long to lift her feet which created a shuffling sound. Doctors, on the other hand, walked hard and stopped abruptly at my doorway before I heard the chart being pulled out and my door being pushed open.

I think my competitive spirit also helped me not get too bored or stressed. Many nights – many, many nights – I would lay there awake in my hospital bed trying to figure out how to get my left hand to move again. I am still grateful for the two doctors who helped me by being brutally honest. One told me, "You may never walk again. We are going to have to wait and see..." Another later said, "You still have challenges ahead of you. If you don't continue to exercise, you will probably end up back in the wheelchair again. Next time it will be a lot harder to get out of it." These men both offered me challenges. My competitive spirit came alive. I was (a) going to walk again and (b) never going back into a wheelchair.

Hospitals have a policy to wheel you out when you are discharged. I fought this tooth and nail. I walked into the hospital on the day of my surgery. When I left, I was determined to walk out and not sit in the wheelchair. I did just that. I walked out on my own. My stress relief came with the determination I would be able to keep up with my young children again someday.

I was at peace from the start. I had my memory. After the surgery, after the stroke, all of my memories remained. Not walking, not hearing, not seeing, not being able to touch things and feel what was there...these things can all be overcome. I had my memories still. From previous experience, I knew I could not have gotten those back if they had been lost. Everything else, I was sure I could learn again. My outlet was this precise challenge – working hard to learn it all again.

Are there ever times when you are not resentful towards your condition? –Megan W.

I don't think there was ever a time I was "resentful" of my condition. Sad – confused – anxious, yes, but I wouldn't say I ever felt resentful.

I remember crying twice after I had my stroke. One time was the night of my ten-year high school reunion. I cried because I was confined to a bed. Half my body was still weak enough that I could not move without assistance. Severe hemiparesis robbed me of my independence. So many simple freedoms were suddenly stolen from me. I couldn't hold my babies. I was frustrated, confused, hurt, and battered only ten years after graduating high school. No one expects that. I cried not for where I should have been that night but where I was at that moment.

It is okay to cry. It is important to grieve for things you lose, but remember it is also okay to laugh. We still need to embrace the gifts which remain. Never stop looking for the unexpected gifts life delivers.

But was I resentful? No, I don't remember feeling resentment. This has truly been a path of recovery and discovery. I left behind what I lost but found ways to make what remains stronger. I embraced the reality that life is short, and we should celebrate everything we have in this moment. *Carpe Diem* – Seize the Day

How did you go about explaining your condition (prosopagnosia) to your children and how did they respond/react? –Hannah W.

My children were not told about me being face blind for quite a while. They were one and two-and-a-half when I had my stroke. It was obvious and unavoidable to let them know "Mom has trouble seeing things" due to the loss of my eyesight. This is all they knew for years. I lost half of my eyesight. Fifty percent of my world is missing with hemianopia. When I couldn't find their teachers, I'd say, "Mom can't see where Ms. Smith is. Can you help me find her?" This was a very typical conversation.

Australian 9News asked that my daughters be on a live interview with me in 2010. I opposed this idea at first. After the producer explained they wanted to create a Mother's Day segment highlighting how even moms with limitations can be great parents, I decided it was the right thing to do.

I took the girls into separate rooms and told them each that I had a problem recognizing faces. They were nine and seven. I let them know I could not recognize them by their faces, but I knew their pretty eyes and loved their smiles. To my surprise, they both responded in the exact same way, "Mom, I know you can't. That's how you've always been." I was shocked. How did they know this? How? Kids just do. Children are more perceptive than we ever give them credit for.

My kids have taken this all in stride. Some children have moms who are horrible cooks. Some moms can't sing a tune to save their bedtime. My kids? My daughters just happen to have a mom who can't recognize people. It is their unquestioned normal. My children love me because they know I will always be there to take care of their needs and offer an immeasurable amount of love.

How has "face-blindness" impacted your relationships with friends and family? –Robert S.

I generally gravitate towards people who have distinctive characteristics. I jokingly say I have the United Nations group of friends. One of the first women I made friends with when we moved into this city was a super tall, super slim lady who always wore a light blue ball cap. She was easy to recognize no matter where I saw her. I need something unique in a person, so I can find them again and again in crowds. My friends are generally outgoing. These people have usually approached me during the initial stages of our friendship.

I don't lead off conversations with, "Look I have this problem with knowing which person you are, so next time I see you..." Many people have difficulty comprehending this within an initial conversation. I am certain I've lost many great friendships before they were given a true chance to get started. Even when I do explain my face blindness, people don't realize the extent of my condition and think I am ignoring them or shying away from conversations. Truth is, half of my world is black due to my eyesight loss. Beyond that, I see every face as a complete stranger. My limitations do not define my relationships with people but, sadly, I am sure prosopagnosia has ended some of them way too soon.

As for my family, prosopagnosia has never affected these relationships. My husband wears a bright-colored ball cap when we go out and my kids stay close by me, but this is the extent it plays into our lives. You do not have to know a face to be able to comprehend the love contained within that person's spirit.

What has your "disability" (for lack of a better word) taught you about the human race? –Lauren C.

I am sure you have heard the old adage, "Don't judge a book by its cover." There is a profound amount of truth to this when you look at other individuals. It is easy to judge people. It's not nearly as easy for us to forego assumptions and focus on what is inside a person's heart. When strangers approach you, judgments often leap into your mind: Their eyes dart too quickly. They are not truthful. Their misfit clothes have been worn too often and are getting holes. They don't have much money. We take neither the time nor effort required to discover what is inside this person.

What have I learned about the human race? There is a lot of good out there in our world. A lot of good. We need to take notice of this good and try not to get pulled into the negativity stemming from quick judgments we too often apply.

Everyone has a story. Every person has a pivotal point or experience that helped shape them into who they are today. Look deeper than what you see at first. Their story may be outrageously funny or horrifically sad. Find these stories and you will better understand who these strangers are. The human race is a beautiful collaboration of people. Even people who have built walls up to protect themselves and lurk in a world of sadness and anger have a warm spirit under that dark shell. People are inherently warm and loving. Be careful not to misjudge what you see in your passing glance. Find their story, and you will better understand them as individuals. Everybody has a story. Every person has a passion and a dream. What is your dream?

Was there a specific event or moment that gave you the courage to share the story of your condition with the public? – Andrea F.

Over the years, I searched extensively for individuals writing and speaking about my four longest-lasting conditions: epilepsy, young stroke patients' recoveries, hemianopia, and prosopagnosia. Rarely could I find first-hand accounts of what it was like to live with these conditions. I did not want to linger in the shadows of scientific studies telling where 28% of patients found this or 68.7% improvement rate was found with that. I wanted to hear from specific individuals who had faced the world and succeeded in living a full life despite limitations.

I knew I had a story to share, and I knew other people could learn from it. It wasn't until two years ago that my hope to share this story became a reality. I am grateful someone saw value in my message and helped me take it to a larger population. A wonderful video was created which helped tell my story. Through this, I had great fortune of becoming friends with a professor and documentary film maker. He has helped me connect with even more people. My story is slowly spreading. The response of gratitude is overwhelming when I realize everything I have experienced is now helping others find their way through a journey of adversity.

My willingness to share my story has nothing to do with courage. This drive to share my experiences stems from being lost and wanting someone to reach out their hand and show me possibilities of a bright future defined by hard work and motivation, not medical challenges. I did not want to be a statistic defined by research found in medical journals and hand-outs in doctors' offices and hospitals. It is my privilege to be able to help more and more people see beyond these statistics. I feel I can now give back and help people realize adversity does not need to take you over and keep you from reaching your full potential. Regardless of the roadblocks, obstacles can be overcome through our use of optimism. Every person has the ability to uncover their inner strengths.

In class you described how your worst nightmare sounded – how did your best dream sound?

My best dream consisted of my hearing happy sounds and feeling gentle touches. I remember the dream vividly. I ran! Running was still a completely unobtainable goal at the time. I had been in physical therapy for over a year, still practicing to walk correctly without the need of any assistive devices. If I tried to walk fast, I fell over nearly every time. I could only stand back and watch my children run and play in the yard at home. I wanted so badly to join them. I often asked physical therapists if they thought one day I might be able to run again. I had an EMG to see if it would be possible in the near future. The results frustrated and saddened me. It appeared the muscle required to allow me to run would probably never redevelop. I felt I had lost the possibility of running ever again.

One morning, due to this dream, I was so happy and felt so free when I opened my eyes. I lay there for a long time trying to find the thoughts which had left me when I awoke. It came back slowly and beautifully. There had been flowers or something soft touching my legs – at that time my left leg still did not have enough sensation to feel soft touches. Yet, I felt this gentle touch brush against me like in a soft, swaying wheat field. I had on a long skirt and laughed as it flowed behind me. I could feel the wind rush against my bare ankles. My children were there laughing and telling me, "Faster, Mommy, faster!" I ran and felt so free. I felt so lucky and happy and my children laughed along with me. We laughed and I ran. That was my happiest dream. That was my best dream. I felt as if my damaged leg was working. I believed my legs could again recognize soft feelings. I heard laughter. I knew I would run again one day.

How long do details stay in your mind? You said you can't remember faces, but you remember things about people. For how long? -Joan K.

Besides not remembering pictures and faces, I have a great memory. When thinking back to your class, I still remember I saw five guys come in wearing ball caps. All but one removed them before class started. The girl in the front quarter of the room near the center had on a very pretty green shirt. Just below the shoulder, the sleeves opened and then closed again half way down her upper arm. The material was light and flowing. In the back of the room about three aisles down on my right, there was a young man sleeping, or resting with his eyes closed, until I finished my conversation regarding the senses I had lost. I was hoping the young lady up top on my left wearing the pink shirt would come down and speak with me. I wanted to see what color her head band was. It was sequined with either dark blue or black. She had very pretty blond hair. I stated these details during class except for pointing out the gentleman who did not remove his cap and the one sleeping. Other than that, ten days have passed and these identifying clues are as clear as the moment you were walking into the room.

"Have you ever sat down and compared your life to that of another "face blindness" patient? If so, did you gain understanding from their perceptions?" –Jeremy B.

I think it's interesting talking to others who have prosopagnosia. Until I did this multiple times, I never quite understood the different degrees – a spectrum of sorts – of severity in face blindness. I've gained a lot listening to how other people handle various situations. Yet, my favorite conversations come from speaking to people who recently discovered they have prosopagnosia. One lady met me and wanted to talk more about this condition. Until she'd seen me on the *Today Show* and then saw a special *60 Minutes*, she never knew it was an actual condition. The relief she felt was obvious and immense. All those years of feeling lost and hearing comments made from others that she was "ditzy" or "not paying enough attention" suddenly washed away. I am fortunate because the Iowa Neurological Patient Registry gave me access to some great researchers who helped me not only put a name to what was going on, but also led me to ways I compensate for abilities I lack.

There is an amazing array of perceptions from both patients and others seeking information about face blindness. I learn something from both groups. They tell their story, and I share mine. Sharing information makes this community, as it does any other, stronger.

Everything I have gone through was an amazing, hands-on learning opportunity for me. It becomes even more worthwhile when I can share these lessons with others.

Conclusion

Do You "Like" Me?

Facebook can cause a lot of confusion for someone who cannot recognize faces. One lady recently asked me to "friend" her. There were hundreds of women with her same name. The next day I went back and told her I couldn't find her. She said, "Just find me by my picture." I responded, "Umm...remember? I am face blind." We had a good laugh.

Realistically, it is an impossible challenge for me. I can look someone up by their name but have no ability to recognize the face on a profile picture. With prosopagnosia, I cannot identify a person a second later let alone when I get home and look up a name in the Facebook search.

To make it easier to connect using social media, I have set up a Facebook page. At **facebook.com/FindingStrengthToStandAgain**, I will have a more successful opportunity to continue conversations with everyone I have met through correspondence and with the wonderful participants who have taken time out of their busy schedules to listen to me speak at various venues. I try to write a quick message every day. Facebook has been a great way for me to stay connected to friends all over the world. I look forward to reading more about you and hearing your thoughts through this connection. Come join me.

Tara loves to engage with her readers. To reach her with questions, comments, or requests for speaking engagements, please write her at findingstrength@rocketmail.com

Made in the USA
San Bernardino, CA
07 March 2018